Reinier Verbeek

Coping with Aggression

How to de-escalate and resolve Conflict

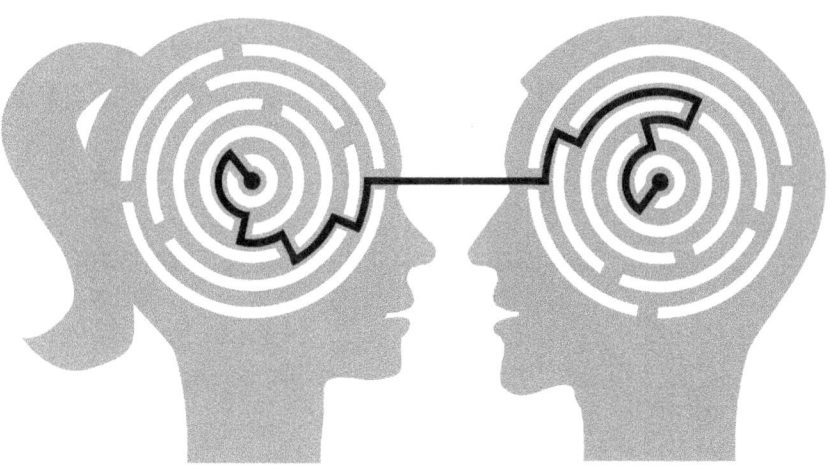

while staying safe during the process

1. Print 05/2024
Published by: R. Verbeek, Austria

ISBN: 9781546393122

CONTENT

Introduction

This book is about how to calm aggressive people, prevent possible dangerous escalations, resolve conflict and stay safe in case of potential physical violence. The content of this book is mainly practically orientated. This should help and benefit a quick transfer into the everyday life of all kinds of readers working in different jobs and performing under sometimes tricky circumstances with high demands, which regularly include dealing with aggressive people and conflicts.

Whenever I personally refer to the concept of "aggression", I do not only mean obvious aggressive behaviour and its typical characteristics that we all somehow know and are familiar with, like intimidations and physical violence. My concept of aggression also implies behaviour not always immediately recognised and categorised as aggression, like passive-aggressive behaviour, negative transferences, and manipulations on all kinds of emotional and mental levels.

My general opinion towards aggression is that the main objective should be to try to deal with it constructively and resolve conflict whilst always staying aware of our personal needs and safety. Moreover, I think it is equally important to get to know our personal tendencies into behaving aggressively, to learn how to channelise stress and negative feelings and be aware of the destructive potential our emotional impulses can have on other people. On the other hand, learning how to use the positive attributes of "aggression" into reaching specific goals, like personal development, building healthy relations and staying safe, could provide real benefits. These positive and beneficial aspects regarding aggression should get more attention too.

The structure of this book

During my professional activities in the army, security services and in (emergency and psychiatric) medical facilities, I learned how specific key elements regarding specially adapted training deliberately prepare and enable people to effectively cope with massive challenges and difficult, potentially dangerous situations. These seemingly different occurrences related to various professional contextual situations all have in common that they put us under a lot of mental pressure. This is caused by the high intrinsic demands found in many such lines of work. In professional realities, the typical, sometimes inevitable challenges can push us to our limits and even exceed our "normal" human capabilities to cope with them.

In the army, but also with the fire department, emergency medical services and a lot of other jobs where a professional standard should be held, and it is important to prevent endangering oneself and others too, it is common to train and even "drill" people according to mentally preparing and practically enabling "process flow-chart" resembling procedures. I am referring to repeating structured, goal-oriented exercises. Because of the usefulness and beneficial effects of this principle of mentally priming oneself and using a "process flow-chart" in dealing with difficult situations, I use this logic structure to train professionals in medical and social institutions. The people working there definitely need to acquire capabilities to professionally deal with conflict, manage aggressive people, and stay safe.

Dealing with aggression can generally be perceived as something purely pragmatic from our point of view. We could only focus on restoring the peace and keeping ourselves safe with all means available like I was used to in the security services. However, sometimes other aspects need to be taken into consideration too. In social institutions, for example, dealing with aggression and even violence is a very delicate process. It also requires understanding mental problems and individual motivations causing this difficult behaviour while always remaining respectful to maintain positive relationships*. Most of the time, these relations were acquired by putting a lot of effort into building them. In social and medical institutions, professional tasks are primarily based and dependent on positive relationships as well. It is a fact that once you have lost people's trust, it is hard to regain. The importance of good conflict resolving and aggression mastering skills is evident.

This book is about this training and mental priming principle of following a "process flow-chart" resembling procedure, as I got to know it. The only difference is that I leave enough room for personal interpretations and suitable adaptations to the specific circumstances and social relationships you could find yourself in. People are different, and there are always more solutions to conflict and turmoil in relationships. Also, aggressive behaviour and conflicts are more fluid and transformative than purely practical tasks like in the army. I use the goal-oriented process flow-chart altogether as a useful guidance tool or basic structure for calming aggressive people and, in the end, and as the most important goal, to resolve conflict.

* In commercial jobs, this isn't much different. Disturbed relations due to unprofessional reactions even towards demanding, difficult customers negatively impact revenue.

I personally remember numerous counts of situations I have found myself being confronted with conflict and aggressive people crossing my boundaries, putting me under enormous pressure and even getting physically violent upon me: on the street, during traffic, at the shop, at work, while performing my job, you name it. As my life progressed naturally and personal circumstances changed, these occurrences under which I encountered aggression shifted.

When I was younger, I experienced situations where I had to deal with massive physical violence during "nights out" in the city. I also had my fair share of scuffles at school, and later on, I was trained to use (armed) violence in the army. I witnessed and experienced the effects of war in Bosnia-Herzegovina and worked at a psychiatric ward in a large city. I even used to be a "bouncer" and dealt with many aggressive, drunk, and violent people. After this period, I trained high-risk security personnel and later medical staff in applying professional tactics and approaches for dealing with violence.

At present, things are somehow different, or maybe my perception has just changed. I now get regularly road cut on the highway, must cope with "dissocial" neighbours and deal professionally with juvenile psychiatric patients who sometimes wholly lose it and need to be "secured" to prevent physically endangering themselves or others. Furthermore, at times conflicts with the parents of those clients take place. Most of the time, these parents themselves behave equally obtrusively and demandingly, but unlike their children, they are seldom officially diagnosed with a mental disease. Even the elderly occasionally can be "aggressive" when they forcefully push their shopping carts into the back of my knees without noticing (or being affected by it). Additionally, in my private life, my children being juveniles and amid an unstable process of building a stable personality, behave demanding and even sometimes aggressively in case of conflict.

All of us have had and are going to have personal experiences dealing with aggression. In some cases, it is even a structural part of a profession. These different circumstances greatly influence the themes and the kind of interactions that will trigger aggression and conflicts. The context will also play a significant role in how one deals with destructive behaviour. It determines the personal tasks, conceptual resources, and the distinct limitations to act. For example, you are walking on the street at night, privately and entirely on your own. Then suddenly, you encounter a drunk person who starts verbally

3

attacking you and becomes very threatening and hostile without any reason. This is an entirely different situation compared to being at work, for example, as a nurse at a psychiatric ward, working for the police or security services. In this context, you have a specific task (which could be dealing with aggression and violence professionally), you are trained in applying certain strategies, and you can depend on colleagues to assist you. Still, even when numerous contextual conditions are of great importance to perceive, understand, and deal with aggression, other distinct elements are always of significant influence, wherever you are.

Whenever you are confronted with destructive and potentially violent aggression, the personal "**I**" invariably assesses and deals with the situation. **You** are the person affected by aggression both on a mental and emotional level. In the end, this determines your actions, even if other people would principally be there to assist you. Support provided by others is, of course, a big help, but not of primary importance, compared to your personal attributes and characteristics. If you find yourself being confronted with an aggressive individual, the following aspects are to a great extent going to determine your reactions:

> ➤ How do I experience this aggressive person and his actions? What is the danger level according to my estimations? Is it still safe to even be here?
> ➤ What are my perceived goals?
> ➤ How do I feel under these circumstances? Do I feel anxious or afraid, and am I even getting angry myself?
> ➤ How high is my stress level?
> ➤ Am I able to control myself, keep myself calm, stay composed and have a clear mind?
> ➤ What can I do? Do I have the necessary skills to cope with aggressive people, or do I feel powerless?
> ➤ How confident am I that I can effectively deal with this situation?

How to de-escalate aggression and resolve conflict

Except for the necessary background information, this book provides five crucial practical steps to effectively deal with aggression and resolve conflict. It mainly depends on your assessment of the situation and the development of the dynamics over time, which measures will be relevant and should be taken to ultimately determine a constructive and safe outcome in the particular process. In some cases, it may only take the first step to channelise your stress reaction. Some challenging encounters again occur suddenly and resolve and dissolve themselves as quickly as they came, and, therefore, require no further actions. On the other hand, you could also find yourself being mentally and emotionally bound in a problematic interaction and entangled in very turbulent and continuously shifting interpersonal dynamics. Then it probably will be necessary to follow and go through all five steps. It could also be necessary to return to take a few steps back and repeat certain steps. Sometimes it is also better to withdraw and leave the scene. Perhaps you were overwhelmed by the situation, or it was required to free yourself from a physical attack like from a chokehold. In the end, it all comes down to the type of encounter, the realistic danger level and how the situation can be dealt with on a personal level. We all have unique personality traits and characteristics. These are important and enable or limit us to remain calm and focused and deal with all kinds of possible encounters. These limitations and capabilities depend on the actual acquired, practical skills and even daily moods and stress levels. And then sometimes people with the best practical abilities and tons of experience in dealing with mental pressure and danger can have bad days too or could get caught by surprise by, for example, a provocation. We are human and will never be 100% perfect.

Feelings of guilt caused by a perceived failure should only be sustained for a short while. Otherwise, it will inhibit us from improving our performance based on lessons learned from past experiences, which can also consist of so-called "failures".

The five practical steps to resolve conflict and de-escalate are:

➢ Regulate stress. Use the heightened performance level to your advantage
➢ Assess the situation and (intuitively) distinguish the form of aggression you are confronted with
➢ Adjust your mental attitude to balance out the current form of aggression and to stay safe
➢ Use verbal de-escalating techniques to resolve conflict as soon as you are on eye level, and agitated people have calmed down
➢ Review and digest your experiences

Step 1:
Regulate acute stress

Step 2:
Identify the form of aggression

Step 3:
Adapt by choosing the appropriate attitude

Step 4:
Apply negotiating techniques

Step 5:
Conduct a debriefing

The Situation

To explain the different steps for de-escalating or balancing aggression, resolving conflict, and keeping you safe, I determined a recognisable starting point based on (for some people) everyday reality. In this case scenario you are suddenly confronted with an agitated, aggressive and hostile person. At first, you see no possibility to avoid this encounter, and you are in the midst of it all. These situations can and will happen, as we all know from our personal experiences from driving our car, shopping in the mall or executing our profession. In this specific, realistic scenario, preliminary warning signs have not been noticed. We possibly did not pay enough attention to warning signs and our intuition trying to raise and direct our attention to the problems and possible danger at hand, which would have enabled us to anticipate and stay in control ahead of the situation's unfolding. Being unaware of subtle feelings and warning signs and failing to respond according to one's intuitive assessment is likely to happen and, I am afraid, is, in fact, usual nowadays. We are sort of "embedded" in a stressful world and exposed to many distractive forces binding our attention and leaving internal subtler cues and feelings unnoticed. These cues and internal signals would otherwise possibly direct our attention towards developing events before they get out of hand. In short, you are suddenly confronted with an unfavourable situation, and you are forced to act upon this situation.

One can only try to prevent conflicts, difficult confrontations and to prepare oneself for various potentially perilous eventualities. Conflict and aggression will inevitably cross your way depending on the (professional) circumstances you are in. Other occurrences will happen, regardless of whether you try to avoid them or not. The "when" and "how" always will be more or less unpredictable, like human behaviour in general. The fact is that these difficult, sometimes borderline dangerous encounters are mentally challenging. When confronted with conflict and aggression, psycho-emotional and energetic mechanisms instinctively prepare us to cope with these situations and keep us safe.

Forceful impacts of aggressive behaviour are generally perceived as unfavourable for maintaining our personal physical and psychological integrity and sometimes are experienced as being threatening to our life. Encounters with aggressive people due to conflict, therefore, lead to a build-up of stress and anxiety and can even cause high levels of tension and the experiencing of real fear. This is a result of stress reactions that are automatically being triggered due to primitive survival mechanisms. With these high levels of stress and the typical related strong emotions, people tend to lose their self-control and start behaving impulsively. When dealing with aggression, this can have disastrous consequences and seldom leads to a positive outcome.

Suppose we want to be able to resolve conflict and deal with aggression and challenging situations that could potentially become dangerous. In that case, we must control ourselves and regain our composure when it is lost. By doing so, this heightened performance level, being an accompanying positive effect of stress, could even be used to our benefit; it enables the clear focused perception of the whole situation, a de-escalation of progressive, destructive dynamics by effective interventions and the prevention of increasing the danger, which could occur if we were to act impulsively. By using stress to our advantage, one can also better assess (intuitively) any potential hazards to adapt the behaviour accordingly. It is also good to realise that in case of an excessive danger level or when people become violent, instinctive reactions and even flight-fight reflexes usually help us to stay safe.

Even when trained extensively in dealing with aggression, stress will always influence our behaviour in both negative and positive ways. Suppressing stress-related reactions, trying to always stay in control, and even repressing feelings and emotions is not the intention of this book. It generally never should be a goal. Whenever a fight-or-flight reaction has been provoked, there usually will have been good reason for that. This means something challenging and possibly dangerous has been (unconsciously) perceived. Maybe afterwards, when you have calmed down and have found the necessary time and space (together with co-workers or other people involved) to think about what happened, it is possible to perceive the experiences more clearly and evaluate the circumstances more rationally. These moments in which you reflect and think provide personal (and professional) learning experiences. These insights are of benefit for coping with future encounters.

1. Conflict, aggression and the effects of stress mechanisms

Stress is a primitive, psycho-physiological mechanism enabling us to anticipate and deal with real dangers (violence, accidents) and insecure situations (tests, professional tasks). These occurrences are also known as "stressors". These different stressors all have in common that they put us under pressure due to their implicit (subjective) meaning. This meaning is formed by the predominant unconscious information processing provided by real-time interactions with our surroundings and other people. However, thoughts and phantasies considering past and future situations can also create stress based on building meaningful mental pictures. These meanings themselves can be determined as being "favourable" but also as "unfavourable". This assessing and constantly differentiating between favourable and unfavourable circumstances is how we function and interrelate with our environment. It is the human principle to sustain life. In the early days of humankind, these mechanisms provided us with safety, saved us from bodily harm and helped us survive. Nowadays, the unfavourable situations we have to deal with are mostly less life-threatening than they used to be. However, these archaic principles are still active in our system and largely determine our actions as we find ourselves confronted with our modern life work-related and interpersonal "stressors".

Once a particular unfavourable situation is identified, the stress hormones adrenalin and nor-adrenalin rapidly build up physical excitement. This sudden increase of bodily energy makes it possible to act upon or cope with these "unfavourable" occurrences. If the stressor cannot be thoroughly dealt with, a different stress hormone (cortisol) will sustain this high level of excitement. This prolonged stress caused by cortisol is common these days because the challenges at our work, for example, cannot be completely dealt with due to their nature. This psycho-physiological mechanism, as described before, is also known as a "stress reaction" or "flight-or-fight reaction". A stress reaction has an enormous impact on both an energetic and an emotional level and significantly alters our conduct. It causes an increase of the blood flow in the brain and results in increased vigilance, focus, sensory perception and attention. The heart function increases and the blood pressure rises. As a result, the muscles are provided with additional oxygen and fuel to burn. Anxiety, fear and anger significantly change our willingness to act. The muscles tense up, and this allows us to respond reflexively if needed. On the other hand, the sensitivity for painful stimuli will decrease, and the bodily excitement raises the body temperature, which is then compensated by sweating.

Individual stress curves

Except for an acute "stress reaction", a certain level of performance is constantly being delivered depending on the tasks and challenges we face. Daily requirements, duties and tasks are commonly not experienced as acute stressors. They, therefore, do not trigger automatic flight-or-fight reactions in comparison to (subjectively perceived) highly uncertain situations and dangers of all kinds that immediately put us on high alert. So generally, over some time, let's say during 24 hours, a changing curve like power output is being delivered. This performance curve consists of highs and lows depending on daily demands as they occur. This curve represents a regular and healthy alternation between delivering performance and recuperating or resting from the efforts made under everyday circumstances.

A stress reaction triggered by an unfavourable, highly challenging situation would result in the ultimate peak performance level an individual can deliver under the influence of these stress hormones. After reaching this peak, a further increase of bodily excitement would not benefit but instead hamper the capability to perform adequately. At and past this point, people tend to lose control, and as a result, their actions become impulsive, chaotic and ineffective. This principle is also known as the Law of Dodson and Yerkes.

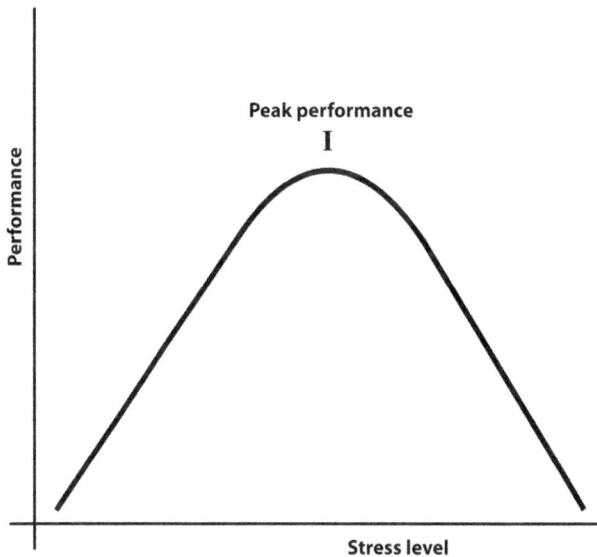

Peak performance

I

Performance

Stress level

1.1. With the building up of physical excitement, our performance level initially increases, reaches a peak and after this, our capacity to adequately deal with challenges declines.

After a stress reaction and when a lot of energy has been dissipated, a natural recovery phase or recuperation occurs typically. It is not possible to deliver this kind of high level of performance without limitations. The energy reserves that are released will be exhausted eventually. Prolonged high demands, often self-imposed due to, for example, professional ambitions, generally have the same effect and drain us from energy equally if we do not rest and recuperate to regain our strength and let off stress hormones (cortisol). After some time, the adverse effects caused by the suffering from bodily and mental exhaustion make themselves noticeable by unwanted physical (impaired immune system, illness), psychological (insomnia, burnout) and behavioural symptoms (agitation, addiction). Therefore, dealing with massive challenges and performing on a high level during a prolonged time without integrating phases to recuperate from the stresses and strains should be avoided.

Impulsive behaviour caused by a flight-or-fight reaction

In the event of a sudden violent attack, instinctive flight-or-fight reactions are crucial. However, these instinctive mechanisms can also cause problems and possibly create dangerous situations due to our responses. They can lead to impulsivity in both acute and less hazardous situations. When dealing with problematic but not by definition dangerous aggressive behaviour and conflict, it poses real problems when people start behaving impulsively. Then instincts and emotions will determine the course of action. As a result, people are not in touch with the actual situation and are going to respond inattentively and probably inadequately and unprofessionally. In most cases, this leads to an escalation instead of de-escalation and resolving of conflict. Dealing effectively with aggression requires us to be in touch with the occurrences as they are and not let our primal instincts get a grip on us. Sometimes, impulsive, instinctive reactions are critical, for instance, if it is required to act immediately in case of violence. Other impulsive actions, however, are inadequate. This means we are overreacting. It can, however, be learned how to channelise these inevitable stress reactions. In doing so, you also get acquainted with how to use this heightened performance level to stay focused and act decisively.

Stress reactions are triggered by combinations of perceived challenges (the estimated danger level of a situation) and the timeframe in which the dynamic develops (How suddenly are you being confronted with aggression? Is it a slow build-up of tension in the dynamics, or is somebody suddenly becoming aggressive without you having noticed any preliminary warning signs?). These factors imply the necessity of a specific "matching" performance level. Our existing capabilities to deal with these kinds of situations (self-defence, negotiating techniques etc.) and strategies for coping with increasing mental pressure will ultimately determine how we handle these challenges; controlled and effective or impulsive, chaotic and ineffective.

The triggering of a flight-or-fight reaction is based on fundamental mental pictures. The brain processes information in the blink of an eye and delivers an assessment much quicker than usual to make it possible to react instinctively and reflexively. Conscious thought processes and focused attention, on the other hand, would provide much more precise and clear assessments. Instinctive reactions are not based on so-called "differentiated mental pictures" and do not require attention to detail. Flight-or-fight responses further lack reflecting capabilities that would benefit balanced decision-making and responses. Using the cerebral cortex, we can generate detailed pictures and reflect on our interventions before we execute them would require taking a longer "route" in our brain. It, therefore, requires relatively more time (approx. 2 seconds) to process information. In short, as long as you are not dealing with acute dangerous situations, you should try to pause two seconds before you react to let your brain work in your favour. This pausing also interrupts the act-react cycle, which is typical for challenges in relations, like conflict and aggression. Pausing can even bring negative interactions immediately to hold and create instant possibilities for solving conflict, as you are not fulfilling counterproductive expectations of opponents. Instead of reacting, you can deal with the situation from your (first-person) perspective according to your personal goals.

Except for dealing with imminent dangers, stress reactions offer a potentially significant advantage; the increased performance level and heightened sensory perception can be used to assess situations more precisely and to exert a more effective, powerful influence with pinpoint interventions. However, the ability to use the heightened performance level will depend on the capability to regulate bodily tension and emotions. The build-up of stress and intense feelings will put us under enormous mental strain. Even when you usually can control the stress hormones, an impulsive, emotional reaction could suddenly be triggered, depending on the dynamics and the way you feel that specific day.

Stress is a large topic on its own. There are many other relevant, exciting facets to be considered and paid attention to. It is essential to raise your awareness concerning these stress-related mechanisms to prevent unwanted reactions and unprofessional behaviour. Therefore, it is generally vital to gain a good insight into one's tendencies when one comes under the influence of stress and experiences mental pressure. Becoming more aware of the typical (body) signals indicating steeply increasing stress levels pose a considerable advantage. It may also be fascinating to raise your awareness of the emerging sensations you experience when you are soon about to overreact and what specific kinds of circumstances (stressors) impact you.

To compare and have a point of reference, it is also important to know how it feels to be in a relaxed and balanced state of mind. Most people, unfortunately, lack this primary point of reference. In jobs with structural high demands like dealing with aggression, you eventually get used to chronic stress, gradually losing the relatedness to a balanced state of mind. However, it can and will lead to unwanted psychological and mental medical conditions and discomforts, which are often being neglected or not being openly discussed.

Step1: Regulate stress and use it to your advantage

Whenever you feel people are behaving aggressively towards you, this means that to some specific extent, your physical and/or psycho-emotional boundaries are under pressure and/or have been crossed. A confrontation with aggressive behaviour causes internal pressure, distinct negative feelings* (anxiety, anger, fear and absolute panic) and often impulsive fight-or-flight behaviour. Even people who initially were affected by aggression could react overly offensive out of an impulse due to the influences of a stress reaction.

The degree to which these sensations occur largely depends on the following factors:

> the perceived risk and danger level
> the availability of practical coping strategies

To channelise our stress levels, to be able to control strong emotions and hence to prevent impulsive reactions, specific practical techniques need to be applied, as are offered to you in this book. These applicable principles compensate for the adverse effects of stress and make it possible to use the positive aspects of a heightened stress level to our benefit. This allows us to influence the dynamics efficiently and to prevent situations from getting worse than they already are. Controlled high levels of stress even allow us to withdraw from a situation in a controlled manner if it gets too dangerous. Suppose the resolving of the conflict, de-escalating of aggression, and staying are our professional goals and requirements. In that case, it is absolutely necessary to apply proven practical techniques to stay in control, compose ourselves, and keep relatively calm and mentally stable, even when the internal pressure is very high.

* The fact that "aggression" is generally associated with negative feelings and stress is also the reason why most people are not eager and motivated to voluntarily contemplate this theme, even when the "darker" sides of human existence can teach a lot about oneself and the relations to other people. Directed attention and positive learning experiences towards considering aggression and integrating personal, commonly more negative connotations and traits of aggression build a strong foundation for enjoying the so-called brighter sides of life.

Basic principles to regulate stress

Keeping at arm's length distance

The first primary step in keeping and regaining situational awareness is establishing the proper distance towards the aggressor. Stressed out and aggressive people usually tend to (or are allowed to) come too close for comfort. Often people are caught by surprise when their boundaries are being crossed because preliminary signs of imminent aggression have not been registered, or sometimes typical cues are ignored. Hence, you can easily find yourself caught and bound in an unexpected predicament that grabs you in an emotional and energetic "chokehold" and won't let you go until you adapt and overcome by taking the proper actions.

With most aggression, the physical distance between those involved reduces rapidly, and both parties end up being in too close of proximity to each other. As a rule, remind yourself that it is too dangerous to remain in this position because you are within someone's physical reach of hitting you instantly. In most cases, indeed, you do not have to fear immediate physical violent attacks. More often, aggressive individuals "just" want to intimidate, or they get themselves into this position as a result of their impulsivity, and they are entirely unaware of this themselves. However, being in close range and striking distance is generally not advantageous for keeping calm, regaining control, and actively de-escalating the situation. This unfavourable situation of being in the striking distance has to be improved by acting assertively.

To adjust unwanted behaviour like the crossing of personal boundaries and, therefore, creating distance towards an aggressor, you can use different levels of interventions. Each intervention level represents an increased intensity of addressing an aggressor to adjust his behaviour and alter his demeanour. It depends on your personal assessment, the person you are dealing with and the state he is in, what intervention level will be needed and applied. The way somebody reacts to these different interventions is a good indicator of what you are dealing with. These interventions are also applicable when dealing with other kinds of behavioural challenges, like the damaging of property.

Firstly, by taking one calm and confident step backwards (this is not the same as taking a step backwards out of insecurity and fear), you will usually regain sufficient physical and psycho-emotional distance to start to de-escalate the situation (first level neutral intervention). If an aggressor doesn't react appropriately, you could also verbally emphasise your need for personal space ("I want you to keep distance from me.") with a semi stretched arm at breast height and signalling a stop sign with your hand(s) towards the aggressor (second level defensive intervention). Additionally, the aggressive individual is signalled that he stepped too close, and you **want** him to keep more distance from you: You assertively claim that you want this person to respect your personal boundaries. Sometimes you need to repeat this message because agitated people predominantly suffer from tunnel vision. The brain then needs some additional external input to understand what you want. If someone still comes too close, it can be necessary to demand this person to keep distance (third level offensive intervention).

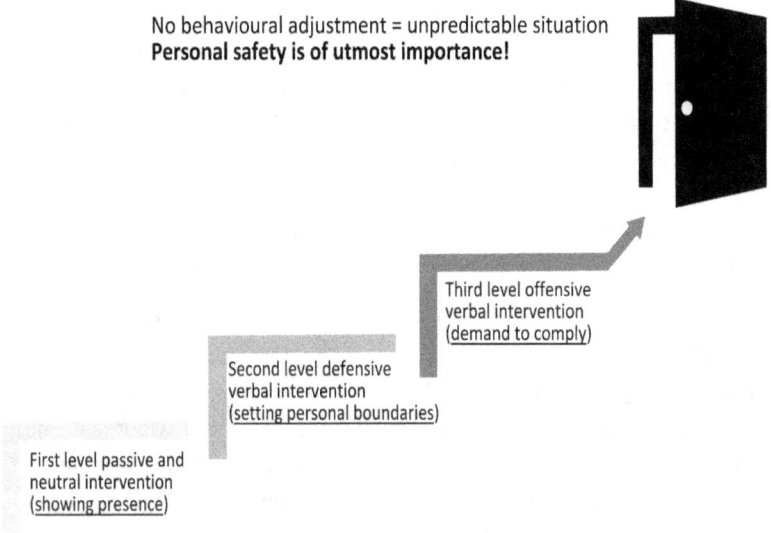

No behavioural adjustment = unpredictable situation
Personal safety is of utmost importance!

Third level offensive
verbal intervention
(demand to comply)

Second level defensive
verbal intervention
(setting personal boundaries)

First level passive and
neutral intervention
(showing presence)

Levels of Interventions, R.Verbeek

As soon as the "normal" distance has been restored by stepping back in a self–confident way or claiming your boundaries and people adjust their behaviour, you could immediately apply verbal de-escalating techniques and redirect the interpersonal dynamics (**Step 3**) to resolve the conflict (**Step 4**). It will also generally provide a better overview of the situation. It will make it

16

easier to "read" this person and detect any tell-tale body signals still indicating hostility and imminent danger. These normally well-recognisable cues are important because they could warn you in time and enable you to anticipate any future potential hazardous move the aggressor might make. This will help keep you safe. Being in this position with sufficient physical distance is generally less stressful for both people as well. The mental pressure automatically decreases as soon as you have removed yourself out of striking distance and the acute danger zone. A real positive effect of a reduced or lower tension level is that it will be easier to keep calm and stay in control and, therefore, prevent impulsive actions on your behalf. Try for yourself what the meaning of personal space is in the next practical experiment, even if going through the process may seem somehow awkward at first.

An experiment

It would be best if you had a partner for this **experiment**, such as a colleague. They should take in an aware, but passive role on this occasion. This person (the more intimate your relationship is, the less this experiment will work) positions right in front of you at about two metres. Now slowly, but progressively, close in towards your partner from the front. During the process of closing in, they should indicate if and when they sense that they feel a shift in their bodily sensations, their awareness of you and maybe that you're getting too close. At what distance have you received a (reflexive) signal from your partner that they sense something was shifting in their awareness and you came too close? Mostly, this will be at an arm's length. This is the actual distance representing the security zone (combination of the intimate and personal sphere). The next step is to move even closer within the security zone and to look straight at them. Describe what you are concretely able to see visually? How is your visual perception of your partner? Are you suffering from tunnel vision? What is left of your peripheral vision? Then reposition yourself by slowly moving backwards until you have reached an arm's length distance (intimate zone) and look at them again. How is your visual perception now? Do you notice this big difference?

With this initial step of actively re-establishing a safe distance, you can more likely channel stress, for example, with simple but very effective breathing techniques. Also, remind yourself that if an aggressor disrespects your verbal and nonverbal signals to keep a safe distance from you, this is a severe indication of this situation's aggressive potential and danger level.

Warning signals like ignoring demands (<u>third level intervention</u>) to keep distance should bring you to a state of high alert. Sometimes this is a good hint that it will be necessary to defend yourself or, even better, to withdraw from this occasion, ideally in a controlled fashion.

A significant advantage of keeping an arm's length distance is that when somebody is going to attack you, this person needs to get in your vicinity by closing in physically to be able to hit you. An imminent attempt to launch a physical attack could be registered by the distinct nonverbal signals the aggressor always sends out. However, these cues can only be noticed as long as we are not completely in a trance-like, fixated state of mind, suffer from tunnel vision, or look down like many people tend to do if they feel insecure. By having this basic overview and catching these tell-tale cues with our senses, our instincts can instantaneously react to these attacks. The brain is basically "fed" with this critical information. Now general defensive measures like creating even more distance, looking for a way out, the blocking of striking arms, the deflecting of chokeholds and the grabbing of clothes by the aggressor is more likely to take place instinctively, and you do not end up being entirely caught by surprise and therefore reacting defencelessly.

Exercise one: your personal security zone

In this exercise, you can follow your basic routines of shopping, working, travelling etc., but, in this case, with heightened sensitivity and awareness of the actual distance people keep toward you. This means practically that you critically observe how close (unfamiliar) people physically move in toward you and how close they position themselves near you. Another aspect of this exercise is to reflect what kind of distinct feelings or sensations this positioning close to people leads to. Bear in mind that the type and quality of relation you have to this person, the general perception concerning this individual, and the specific context drastically influence the effect. You could also try to become aware of your tendencies considering reactions whenever you feel people are positioning themselves too close. It can be quite interesting to "observe" and self-reflect on your feelings and behaviour. These "automatic" reactions can widely differ. You can, for example, start to feel anxious, uncomfortable and still not change your position. However, you could also move away from this person and reposition yourself and, at the same time, look for trustworthy people you can "accompany" by (unconsciously) creating an opportunity to be in their vicinity.

General description of a situation:
Which feelings or internal sensations did this cause?
How did I react?

*Additional exercise templates can be found on page 137

Some aspects to consider

Always keep an escape route open and available

By keeping an escape route open and available, it will always be possible to leave a situation securely whenever it becomes too dangerous to try to intervene, and it starts to get out of hand. It is also going to make you generally feel safer. The availability of an escape route positively affects the build-up of stress compared to being blocked in a confined space like a room or alley, etc. However, whatever counts for you certainly will count for an emotionally charged, wound up and aggressive individual. The availability of an escape route gets even more relevant in case you appear on the scene with additional people while not being aware you are unconsciously applying extra pressure onto this person, who, like in most cases, behaves aggressively out of anxiety and stress. It is seldom advantageous when an escape route is blocked or an agitated and angry individual is driven into a corner. The tension will further increase, and impulsive, defensive attacks become more likely. Therefore, one of the golden rules is always leaving a flight path open for both parties. This isn't always easy depending on where you are, how big or small a room or space is, how many people are involved and what options are available. It is mandatory to remain critical and constantly situational aware, even when the inevitable effects of stress will not make this easy.

One is none; two is one

Always at least try to get a **second person** to join you as a **backup** whenever you are dealing with an aggressive individual. Two people working together as a team can support and complement each other both on a physical and on a psychological level. A second person, acting like a supplementing partner, reduces our anxiety and stress. This allows you to stay composed longer. It is easier to keep calm under pressure and assess the situation with less emotional bias when not acting solely by yourself. You probably feel more confident, and, therefore, the interventions are going to be more effective. It is also generally more secure to deal with aggressive people if somebody is available to watch your back. An exception to this rule is, of course, whenever another person, a colleague, for example, is fuelling the dynamics and contributing to the situation negatively. The function of a partner is to act as a backup, provide basic physical security, and help you defend against all kinds of physical attacks if needed. He or she can also get additional help or alarm important people and instances, like the police or security services.

Sometimes it is not possible to effectively de-escalate a situation when perhaps you cannot connect and relate to the aggressor, or this individual has a persisting negative attitude towards you and projects frustrations and anger. Remaining in this position and not being able to build a relationship can make a situation more difficult and could cause it to escalate. In these specific cases, it is better to "step back", change roles, and let somebody else try to connect to this person constructively.

"Changing roles" allows you to create an appropriate distance to the situation on an emotional level, and it is going to be less likely that impulsive reactions out of frustration will occur in case a discussion is non-productive. Your partner can take over with a clear mind and probably fill in a more positive role. The chances are good that changing positions will quickly have a de-escalating effect. Most aggressive people look for a way out and are not "happy" to be in this predicament either. This principle of using roles with different meanings is also known as the "good cop versus bad cop strategy".

People under stress and emotional pressure have a hard time differentiating relations with other people than when they are in a relatively balanced state of mind. This differentiation is based on the meanings that associations have, which are related to the individual representations of personal needs like, for example, feeling safe, being respected and experiencing friendship. Anxious, agitated and angry individuals can no longer differentiate in "colours" regarding the meanings of interactions with others, as they probably would be able to do under normal circumstances. Due to stress, they are only able to differentiate in "black" and "white" or "good" and "bad" qualities of meanings and are projecting these undifferentiated mental images onto other people, like us. Under the influences of high internal pressure, the perception of occurrences of most people is limited to discern between, on the one hand - "unfavourable", "potential risk" and "danger", and on the other hand - "favourable", "security" and "safety". It is essential to be aware of this fact whenever you're dealing with aggressive people and conflict.

Practical techniques to regulate stress

Due to a stress reaction, everything seems to transpire enormously fast, and there appears to be no time to reflect, think and then act. Sometimes this is indeed the case, and it is required to (re-)act immediately without hesitating. On the other hand, there will be a broader timeframe available to reflect and choose the most suitable strategy in many situations. Practical stress regulating principles help in "finding" and re-establishing this perception of a more general timeframe.

There are different techniques to channel stress. Concrete breathing techniques are very effective and are quite easy to do. They are helpful if you find yourself being confronted with acute challenges which you cannot avoid. These intense challenges can be when you are suddenly opposing a hostile intimidating or provocative person or in case you are aggressively being cut off by a car. Often, we are caught by surprise by all sorts of challenging situations. These sudden moments can be overwhelming, and in the blink of an eye, you can suffer from tunnel vision - one of the main psycho-physiological effects of a stress reaction. A tunnel vision is caused by a narrowing down of perception. It is an extreme focusing on the challenges at hand. Due to this tunnel vision, people often react impulsively and emotionally. When dealing with aggression, however, this should be prevented, when possible, as it is counterproductive and makes situations more insecure and even dangerous.

With a stress reaction, bodily tension can be felt rising from the belly/stomach area and creating an energetic "knot-like" sensation in the chest area. Regular breathing patterns are suddenly being substituted for shallow and rapid breathing patterns, which is a typical indication of increasing physical and mental pressure. The whole system is getting in a state of readiness and prepares itself to act upon the challenges at hand instinctively. By breathing out with pressed lips and taking one deep breath or even better, by taking two or even more deep breaths and by breathing normally from the belly after this sequence of taking deep breaths, you can prevent getting tunnel vision and regain the perception of a broader timeframe and control your emotional impulses. You could also combine this simple but effective breathing exercise (breath out...and breath normally) with a movement like stepping backwards, as I described earlier. Then you mentally and physically create more distance towards the challenges and prevent suffering from tunnel vision.

This easy principle, which only needs a little practice and is integrated quickly because the effects are enormous and noticeable, allows you to stay grounded. Your peripheral vision is restored, and the perception of the challenges becomes a differentiated quality again. This has to do with reducing mental pressure and the extra two seconds our brain is given to process information. Neurologic processes are provided with the short but necessary time to reproduce detailed pictures of the challenges you face. This gaining of time also allows the brain to find adequate strategies to adapt to and deal with, in this case, aggression. Breathing out and then deeply in for one, two or more times followed by regular breathing instead of cramping and breathing shallowly from the chest makes it likelier that you remain calm under stress. Breathing techniques are ideal because they also allow you to use the stress-related heightened performance level to your advantage; it will enable you to reflect and perceive clearly what is happening so you can act more effectively. In real danger, it is also more secure to stay calm and find a way out in a controlled fashion. If a sudden attack takes place, primary instincts will be triggered anyway. Instincts are there to protect you from harm and function beyond our control.

A very effective technique to regulate stress and mentally guard yourself against negativity is to deliberately direct your attention away from the challenges at hand and not to hyper-focus on aggressive people, etc. After you realise you are facing challenges like a conflict or aggressive behaviour, and you gain an arm's length distance, if needed, it helps to redirect your attention towards your upper body and try to feel with which part you are predominantly breathing with. Is it your belly or your chest? **Concentrate for two or more seconds and try not to immediately react to situations if it is not required (which mostly is the case).** Often, we feel we need to respond, but this is nothing but a product of your own aspirations and, even more often, of anxiety. The main goal of these initial impulsive reactions is to control the situation and people. You can also shift your attention and focus onto the lower part of your body, like your hips, legs or especially feet. It helps to stay grounded and hence with yourself. These techniques help to reduce the internal pressure effectively and to remain composed. You still will observe the situation, but you are no longer hyper-focusing and absorbing your opposite's negative tension and emotions.

Summary

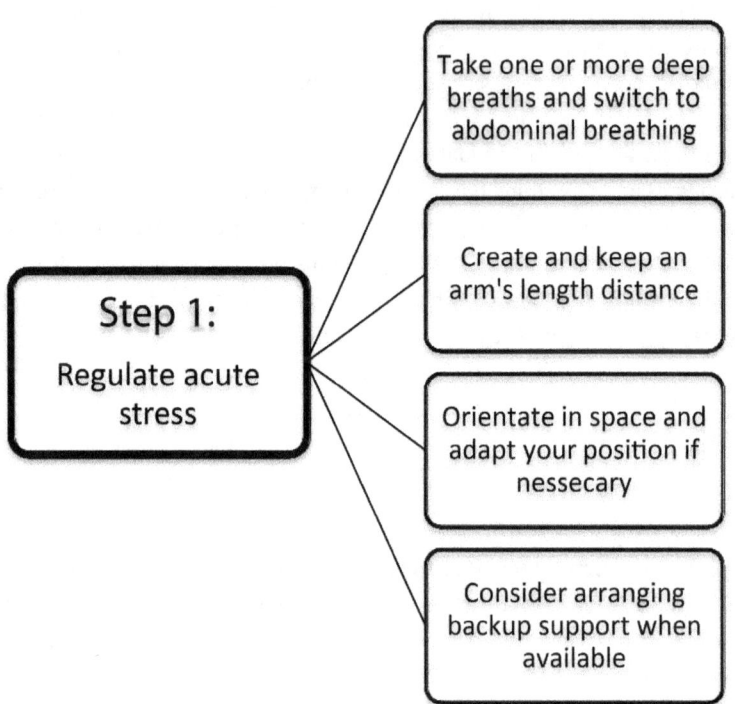

Exercise two: channelling and using stress

This is an easy and basic breathing exercise. I suggest you just sit down on a chair, couch or whatever is comfortable for you. You may, of course, also lay down flat on a thin mattress on the ground and completely relax your body. If in a seating position, place your feet flat on the floor and straighten your back. Your arms may rest on your lap during the process. It is important to relax your muscles and sit comfortably, without putting any strain on your body and without being disturbed by any distracting noises, running computers, cell phones, etc. Now, while being in this relaxed position, you calmly direct your attention to your breathing pattern without actively trying to influence it. Just observe and feel how you breathe in … and breathe out.

After a while, ask yourself this question: "Do I breathe from the chest or belly area?", "Where is it that my breath comes from?" If the answer is that you are breathing from the belly area, then continue the process of connecting to your breathing pattern by completely directing your attention towards it. If you tend to breathe from the chest area, shift and try to breathe from the belly area, which means that your belly will expand and flatten repeatedly. A flattening diaphragm, which divides your lung cavity from your abdominal cavity, creates a negative pressure in your lungs, and therefore, the air gets sucked in. When breathing out, a bulging diaphragm pushes the air out of your lungs.

While observing and sensing this breathing process, ask yourself these questions: what happens inside of me, how do I feel, what bodily sensations emerge? Do I feel the tension drop inside of me? Most people start to feel their legs more pronounced and become more aware of the bottom of their feet and sense the surface structure of the ground below their feet. These effects are typical for conscious and attentive breathing exercises. Nothing spectacular, I know, but nevertheless very effective for influencing your state of mind positively. You can combine this exercise with the first one. This means you observe your reactions in case unfamiliar people get too close, and you sense an internal pressure building because of this. Just take a deep breath and calmly concentrate on your breathing pattern. This strategy of paying attention to your breathing also leads the attention "inside" and allows disconnecting from the situation and stressful demands "outside".

Some other practical stress regulating techniques

Deflecting negative projections

In social interaction, people mutually "fill in" a role for their counterparts. This role we like to see others in is based on personal needs. The professional role we play in a specific context often is the reason for conflict and people behaving aggressively. They aim their aggression towards the people in this professional role by projecting negative feelings and images onto them.

If you are in a position or fulfil a particular professional role and people start behaving aggressively towards you, it is likely you immediately react according to the transferred expectations. It is easy to feel provoked and to behave defensively due to the nature of a certain role and the meaning it will also have to us. Sometimes it isn't easy to stay aware of the relativity of the professional position we fill and to keep in mind that we are not being targeted as private persons usually. This isn't easy because we are being affected on a personal level due to the nature of aggressive mechanisms. Conflict and aggression cause stress, anxiety, or even anger, and we tend to react accordingly, even when we do not represent a private person in this professional context.

By using a combination of basic stress-regulation techniques, self-reflecting capabilities, and rationalising the situation itself and not taking it too personally, you can maintain this awareness of the relativity of the part you play. You will be able to perceive the fundamental dynamics as it develops in a more rational, clear perspective. By actively distancing yourself from or stepping out of this role and maybe even by shifting into a different role, it is possible to defuse the negativity directed at you and to de-escalate instantly. This also positively affects your stress level, as you are no longer in this negative position and its high demands.

It can also create an advantage to step out of this negative ("bad cop") role. A partner could help to build this much-needed distance and might even become the "good cop". By pulling this card and creating a positive mirror, people "see" their own negative behaviour, suddenly regulate themselves and even become more cooperative and turn friendly. You could also switch roles and "change hats", so to speak. You then switch from being the bad guy to being the good guy.

By humanising yourself, an opposite person tends to treat you the way he would want to be treated.

Of course, in some situations, it is not possible to step back or switch roles. Occasionally, it will be required to remain in this professional role, and it is necessary to endure this negativity and have a thick skin, considering it is a part of the job. But in a lot of situations, it will be possible to distract and deflect negative projections. Find room for flexibility where possible. Stay firm if needed.

Not always will we be caught by an acute situation in which only the previously mentioned methods for stress-regulation (two seconds rule, breathing out…breathing normally, directing your attention away from the problem) are helpful to stay calm and maintain our composure. Especially in everyday conflict situations and while verbally trying to de-escalate, it will still be possible to use some other very effective techniques, which I will describe later. It is also possible that the initial de-escalating efforts were successfully applied, and valuable time has been gained to reassess what should be the next step to take. Some confrontations are very short-lived. However, after these experiences with aggression, a high level of stress hormones often persists in our system, accompanied mainly by pent-up mixed emotions and undigested negative impressions. The following practical techniques can be used to balance out mental pressure in case you have more time at your disposal or to reduce persisting stress symptoms after you had a negative experience to come to a state of ease.

For some time, I read about a very effective stress-reducing technique in a book called "**Silva Mind Control Method**" written by Jose da Silva. The technique described in this book is applied to influencing brain activity to reach an Alpha-Level state. This is a deficient meditative level of brain activity. This book from Mr. da Silva is about a completely other topic and has nothing to do with resolving conflict or dealing with aggression. It describes how to regain and keep control over your mind, succeed in reaching a meditative state, be mindful, visualise and imagine pictures of personal goals you would like to achieve, and how to create a future reality. The basic concept of this book that I use is the "**counting backwards principle**". This technique by itself impressively succeeds in influencing brain activity and "silencing" the ego. This technique is effortless: you count backwards from 100 to 1 and take a one-second pause between every counting step. So obviously, it is a prolonged attentive process (100-second pause, 99-second pause, 98-second pause......till you reach 1). I would advise visualising the numbers during the counting process too. My experience is that visualising numbers simultaneously makes this technique even more effective (but also more of a challenge, as your mind tends to drift away, and your thoughts can be very intrusive).

As soon as familiarisation with this principle and the positive effects it brings has been accomplished, the program itself could be adapted to make it more efficient. Counting from 100 to one takes too much time and attention in most situations. After you have gained experience with this technique, balanced out chronic stress states, and created a decent base to go from, you could achieve the same calming, relaxing effect on your mental state only by counting from 10 to one. You could, at some point, establish an anchor in mind. Then only remembering this counting backwards principle in a stressful situation could positively affect stress-related symptoms, and no real counting is practically required. This anchor can also be symbolised by and linked to a personal object, like a necklace.

The counting back technique is a very powerful tool to recover from a stress-related negative effect I call the "fragmentation of the mind". This effect occurs due to parallel mental attachments to various, non-related challenges. Counting backwards is very helpful if you desire to re-establish a clear perception, to be focused, mindful and "with yourself". You can restore a connection to and be in the "now" and "see", reflect and sense the implications of envisaged strategies for dealing with current demands. These multiple tasks from which you momentarily disconnect can also be re-organised and put into a new structure or time plan by prioritising and determining what needs to be done first.

Visualising imaginary mental pictures is another suitable method to influence stress-related symptoms positively. This principle enables you to re-establish the connection to yourself, reflect and perceive clearly "what is going on" in your surroundings. Lowering the mental pressure positively influences the perception of a so-called task-relevant "timeframe", too. This frame ultimately determines how much time you will "see", being subjectively available, to accomplish specific tasks and to tackle the challenges at hand. It is best to practise this technique of visualising lucid, imaginary mental pictures in a quiet place, where you remain undisturbed.

The principle is very easy, but it is required to create a distance from the everyday turbulent and noisy surroundings, which are probably common at most workplaces. It is important to arrange a quiet location you can withdraw to, where you can concentrate and direct your attention inward.

The first practical step in the process of visualising imaginary mental pictures is to focus your attention (for now, with your eyes closed) on the area in between your eyes, a little above the level of the eyebrows. This is the position of your (I call it this way) "mental film screen". It is a white screen, without any images being projected on it. This mental (film) screen between your eyes (the only thing that gets your attention now) is a place where all sorts of things can be made to happen. Here you can project (visualise) imagined lucid pictures of places and circumstances associated with past positive experiences, like being at the beach or at home reading, working in your garden etc. Another good alternative is to just visualise yourself being generally in a relaxed and balanced state of mind. What image do you see when you observe yourself standing in front of a mirror while being in a relaxed state of mind and at ease? How do people generally look when they are with themselves and balanced? These "as if" or "I remember that place where I felt so good and relaxed" visualisations influence the state of mind both on a psychological and physical level (tension-reducing) effectively and rapidly.

The brain cannot distinguish very well between actual and construed "realities", like in this occasion of visualised images. As a result, the brain will respond according to these imagined images **as if** they were real. This causes all sorts of sensations and internal reactions depending on whatever you have visualised. Your physical and psychological (emotional) functioning aligns with the visualised pictures on this mental screen. This is your reality now. A positive secondary effect is that as soon as you direct your attention to your inner world, you will create a distance (by a deliberate disassociation or detachment) towards the demands of the "outside world".

You can also use so-called **Affirmations** and combine them with the principle of visualising, as described before. An Affirmation is a phrase starting with the personal pronoun "I", which should consist of specific goal-orientated meaning for the one whose inner voice expresses it. The goal is to influence the state of mind in the present. In this case, this goal is to reduce tension in the "now". To achieve this, you need to use the typical phrases with a relaxing meaning which effectively calm you down.

Affirmations combined with visualisations work even better and are more effective. Examples for affirmations are: "I am calm"; "I keep my distance and keep my calm".

When you start constructing certain phrases or affirmations (in your mind), you will notice that they usually automatically fit your personality and preferences, as these sentences are derived from your personal experiences and knowledge about yourself. The only type of sentences you should not use are the ones that have built-in time limitations or refer to future expectations like: "I am still calm"; "I will regain my calmness". With affirmations, it is all about the "now".

The various techniques I described to regulate stress symptoms are not all that exciting and spectacular, but they are still influential. In the end, whatever technique you will choose to use is a personal decision. This is important because you are the only person who understands and knows what is going to help you stay calm, composed, and in control of the situation. I can only recommend gathering your own experiences by trying them out and finding the technique that fits you the best. What works for one person doesn't always work for somebody else. Acknowledging what works for you will motivate you to use them actively. In actual stressful situations, stress-reducing skills are essential. They build a basis for the following next steps, making it possible to constructively deal with aggression and stay safe.

As soon as you have achieved controlling impulsive reactions, but the situation has not changed, and you are still being confronted with this aggressive person, making it necessary to deal with the situation, assessing the form of aggression is the next step to take. It is crucial to remain aware that a fight-or-flight response could be triggered at all times. You can still lose your self-control, even when you have managed to stay calm at first. Stress-related mental pressure could increase with the progression and development of the dynamics, and, as a result, it can get more challenging to stay composed. In reality, it will often be necessary to repeat stress regulating techniques.

Exercise three: experiencing stress reduction techniques

For this exercise, I suggest you take a comfortable seat in a quiet place without any distracting forces, turn off your phone, etc. Position yourself on a comfortable chair with a straight back with your feet flat onto the ground. You may rest your hands in your lap during the length of the process of this exercise, and you may even close your eyes. Try to remind yourself of the stress-reducing techniques that were described in this book. You can also have a quick look at the table of contents to remind yourself. Which technique immediately draws your attention?

I suggest you try the technique that first came to mind and calmly go through the process of practicing it. After you are finished, please write down your findings when you feel like it. You can tick the boxes to evaluate your experiences and their effectiveness. Then, you could proceed and try another technique. If you sense any resistance, then remember that it makes no sense at all fighting this hard, on the contrary. However, you could also try to acknowledge this resisting force inside of you, have a look at it, smile towards it, accept it and let it go or pass by. If you only find one appealing technique, this is fine, as you cannot apply more than one technique at the same time anyway.

Counting backwards

My experiences with this technique:
Valuation of the effectiveness
Score from 1-10:

Visualising mental pictures

My experiences with this technique:
Valuation of the effectiveness
Score from 1-10:

Affirmations

My experiences with this technique:
Valuation of the effectiveness
Score from 1-10:

2. The theory behind the different forms of aggression

Different forms of aggression can be distinguished by their typical characteristics. These differences are based on the purpose of these kinds of aggression for the aggressor and its effects on the victim and the relationship. The significant advantage of distinguishing between forms of aggression is that each form represents a well-defined so-called mental model. These distinct models can be (intuitively) recalled and used to choose appropriate strategies to adapt to the situation, even if our stress would rise to a high level. Whenever we start to experience stress and become anxious, it is imperative to have explicit referential models at our disposal. It will become likelier that we will then remain in control over ourselves longer. These models represent well-defined structures we sort of can "hold onto" as soon as our brain starts working in overdrive. We will be able to perform professionally even under high mental pressure.

These different forms of aggression also demonstrate that not all occurrences that might appear dangerous by our estimation are hazardous in reality and lead to violence. I often experienced people being unable to discern different types of aggression. They tend to generalise according to their personal experiences and socialisation. This causes them even to panic when there is no sign of imminent danger. This is mainly caused due to the similarity regarding the behavioural cues typical for aggression. In their minds, these cues are always an indication of potential physical violence. In many cases, people cannot differentiate beyond the abstract and often very personal concept of aggression. Most people, even professionals, basically have never learned how to distinguish these differences. On the other hand, people who have experience identifying the different forms of aggression can "read" a realistic danger level.

To distinguish the various forms of aggression at least requires motivation and a willingness to learn. By doing so, you obtain this fundamental skill. I always use situations where I am not actively involved and can observe calmly and reflect on what I might do in the same situation. I also train my brain into differentiating by watching pretty useless reality television or the news. A lot of times, the themes are somehow related to aggression or at least general human behaviour. This often structural, theatrical, dysfunctional behaviour in the case of reality television draws the attention of many viewers, motivating to show these scenes and make such programs. As soon as you have acquired more passive experience, you could also use actual situations to practise and prime yourself and eventually use these abilities better to your own advantage. Conclusions of what has been observed will occur automatically when you have gained some basic knowledge, for example, provided by this book. The quality of your observations may differ, and sometimes you may feel uncertain what it is you are observing. Observations and assessments will always remain personal and sometimes can be biased, especially when emotions come into play. However, by using a combination of the ingredients "knowledge" and "a self-critical mindset", these assessments are going to get a more appropriate professional value and will function as trustworthy heuristics. Then you can instantly recognise the different forms on an intuitive level and confirm your assessment by consciously observing the distinct behavioural cues as a follow-up.

To eventually achieve this skill level, it is vital to inform yourself and reflect and consequently analyse your own experiences after dealing with aggressive behaviour. Ideally, this is done with a competent co-worker, a colleague, or somebody involved in or at the scene. In the chapter about debriefings (**step 5**), I will explain this principle regarding "the processing of experiences". When under massive pressure, you will not be able to analyse and consciously distinguish between different forms of aggression. Then it all comes down to how you have been mentally "primed" by past experiences and to what extent the ability to differentiate is being trained.

Forms of aggression

As destructive interpersonal dynamics progresses over time and tension increases, people's behaviour changes according to their personality traits, (temporary) dispositions and specific circumstances. At lower levels of arousal and agitation, people often act heavily demanding offensively. As soon as the tension increases, they will show hostile, threatening or provoking behaviour. In the eventuality that they completely lose their self-control, the destruction of objects and even the launching of a sudden physical attack are real possibilities.

In some cases, however, imminent aggression cannot easily be distinguished from normal behaviour because there are no observable typical cues and signs. Some people build up high levels of tension due to conflict but manage to control themselves effectively. However, negative thoughts and images of subjective perceived threatening "enemies" are construed during these internal processes. Eventually, this content will be projected onto these perceived "hostile" individuals. These negative projections, accompanied by anger, sometimes feelings of hate and high levels of tension, could eventually lead to a sudden outburst of aggression and even a directed, intentional (physical) attack that victims do not expect to happen and do not see coming. Furthermore, some people plan to use deliberate violence to achieve their goals in a very calm and composed way, like sociopaths and criminals.

Each different form of aggression has a specific function for the aggressor. They are used to (mostly subconsciously) trying to satisfy particular needs. The needs themselves can differ from being obvious everyday ones (for example, getting a "better" seat at the theatre or on the train) to the not so obvious, representing establishing a feeling of personal security by controlling and exerting power on people and situations. However, it gets even more complicated, as these needs are in some way connected; not getting a seat by using, i.e., demanding behaviour, can make people feel anxious and, therefore, lead to an overly aggressiveness as compensation for these negative feelings. The venting of frustration and relieving from chronic stress could be a need, too, to regain an internal balance and stay healthy in the long term. It is often understood as aggressive because of the typical accompanying behavioural cues and the negative way it usually affects people. This so-called "acting out of frustration" can be triggered by the slightest conflict.

Different forms of aggression can be distinguished on a conscious level and more probable in actual situations, on an intuitive or pre-conscious level. The recognition of forms of aggression is possible as soon as behavioural cues are associated and match with a memorised pattern coming with practical experience. Intuition also helps recognise processes of aggressive dynamics in an early stage of its development when people are still controlling themselves but are highly charged with negative energy. Intuition is even of great value if decisions need to be made whenever there is no time to think and analyse what to do, like in the case of aggression. In short, intuition is a great resource and could warn of all kinds of danger at hand. However, what should remain is a critical awareness that intuitive assessments could prove to be biased due to the influence of personal experiences, subjective interpretations, and transferred information or models. On the other hand, rational thinking and analysing also underlie complicated interfering principles, like for example the bending of perceived information and using convenient arguments to create a subjective reality that fits (and does not contradict) personal needs. Our stressful modern-day society makes it harder to use intuition as an actual skill for assessing and becoming aware of situations. The modern world nowadays is full of distractive, and attention-drawing forces. We often lose the ability to be in touch with our (gut) feelings and subtle mental pictures and reflect on what is going on in our surroundings. These features and human traits could effectively warn us before it is too late. Our feelings continuously indirectly indicate what is happening in our surroundings and what ordinary meanings these occurrences personally have on us. But, in comparison to conscious awareness and thoughts, this occurs on a subtle pre-conscious level.

When people desire to be more aware of the processes within and use intuition as a practically valuable tool, most need to adjust certain structural things, and behavioural patterns in their lives to (re-) connect with these levels of our being. To make use of intuition and the benefits it provides, staying focused and calm is generally necessary. Especially in dealing with aggression, taking notice of our feelings and (ideally) relating them to outside events by reflecting consciously gets even more difficult. Stress hormones can be helpful to focus and be in touch with the challenges at hand. The effects of stress might also narrow down our perception and lead to a so-called tunnel vision. Keeping (all kinds of) hormones under control is challenging. We probably all know this by experience.

Regarding distinguishing the various forms of aggression, it is important to remind ourselves that personal assessments are always related to one's traits and experiences. However, with extended and regular training combined with a heightened sensitisation and abilities in critical self-reflection, an apt assessment becomes more probable.

The following categories of aggression are based on the typical functions for the aggressor and the meanings and implications for those affected by them. The chronological order of these forms of aggression represents the level of excitement of the aggressor, the intensity and severity of the impacts these specific aggressive acts have on victims, and the potential risk of physical violence. Each of these factors (intensity, severity and risk level) will increase progressively with each described succeeding category.

Forms of Aggression:

> ➤ Demanding behaviour
> ➤ Invasive, aggressive manipulations
> ➤ Aggressive acts out of frustration
> ➤ Intentional physical violence

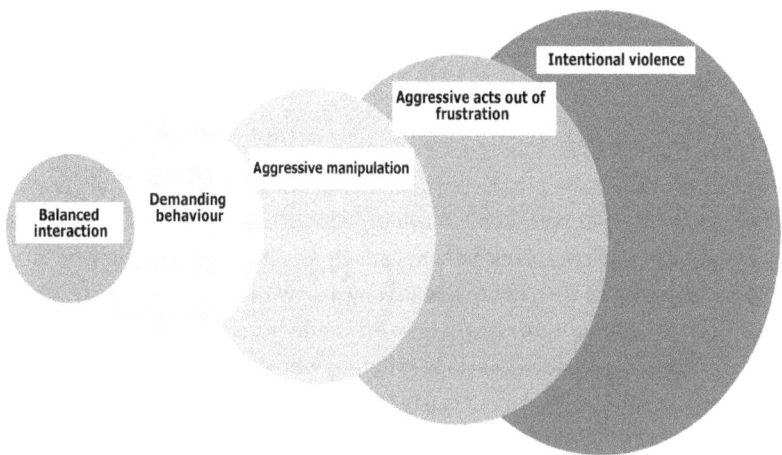

Forms of Aggression, R.Verbeek

Demanding behaviour

With this kind of behaviour, people enforce their personal needs by exerting pressure on others. It is a relatively subtle form of aggression and initially remains unnoticed on a lot of occasions. This has to do with the fact that most people unconsciously tend to go along and cooperate according to the demands.

Demanding behaviour often initiates a progression of negative interpersonal dynamics. On the one side, increasing discrepancies will arise when personal needs are persistently neglected due to this acquiescence. This frustration becomes apparent by the way affected people eventually start to behave like themselves in social relationships. On the other side, the possibility that demanding individuals are going to enforce their wants with even more pressure if people (at first) deny cooperating is relatively large. This happens especially if those individuals are used to dealing with compliant people. This

37

form of aggression bears a considerable potential to initiate massive conflicts and destructive dynamics. Typically, when the relationship with the aggressor continues. At some point, setting boundaries cannot be avoided, and a confrontation is inevitable.

The probability to encounter offensive, demanding people in daily life is considerable. It is much more common than other forms of aggression and represents a large base in the aggression spectrum. The difference to standard approaches in social relationships is substantial, but in most cases, it stays unnoticed until it is too late. With refined sensibility and attention for these mechanisms and awareness of one's boundaries, this form of aggression can be very well detected and recognised. The actual effects of this kind of aggression will be strongly related to the contextual situation and the characteristics of the person confronted with this behaviour. People will react depending on their needs and importance, which are negatively affected by demanding behaviour. Most people often tend not to adequately deal with this form of aggression and wait too long before drawing a line. This influences all kinds of future social interactions in a negative way, for instance, with people who initially were not involved and therefore cannot relate to the negativity and frustrated behaviour they encounter. A build-up of stress and feelings of frustration resulting from harmful confrontations with demanding people are also generally unfavourable for showing de-escalating capabilities and, for example, being patient, staying composed or listening well. However, these adverse effects can be prevented by immediately balancing out this aggression with the proper interventions.

The typical characteristics of this form of aggression

When people behave demanding offensively, they forcefully emphasise the satisfaction of their personal needs at the expense of others. The typical characteristics make themselves noticeable by how these needs are verbally expressed: distinct selfish, mostly repeating demands, the challenging, pushing and urging of others to comply. The messages are being communicated in an aggravated style and expressed in a demeaning, dominating instructing level. The vocal expression is direct, brusque and loud, and it sometimes possesses a distinct hostile quality.

These verbal messages are accompanied by congruent offensive nonverbal expressions:

- ➢ a general offensive posture
- ➢ piercing eyes
- ➢ a fixated stare
- ➢ increased muscle tone (in the neck area)
- ➢ outstretched arms
- ➢ a rigid way posture caused by an internal build-up of tension

Demanding individuals also tend to position themselves too close to others in their personal and intimate sphere and often make a distinct step forward to apply even more pressure. They often could even grab hold of the clothes of a victim.

This form of aggression can be distinguished from average assertiveness shown in relationships due to the pronounced persisting offensive quality of behaviour and the crossing of personal boundaries. As a result of the exerted pressure, the personal needs of those confronted with this aggression are implicitly denied. This form of aggression can make people feel anxious, and some even feel intimidated because a demanding person takes up a lot of space regarding his personal needs. They tend to "corner" their victims. Nevertheless, demanding behaviour has the most negligible severe effects and destructive potential in comparison to the other forms of aggression like, for example, aggressive intimidations.

What effect does this form of aggression have on us?

If confronted with this kind of aggression, sooner or later, you will start to feel massively pressured. Offensive demanding is stressful to deal with, and you will likely react out of frustration at some point. As I said, how one reacts to such stress depends entirely on the person affected by this aggression and the situation he is in; where one person responds very strongly to this aggression, another can keep his calm. Demanding behaviour will have different individual meanings depending on personality traits, unique (work-related) ambitions and contextual circumstances. It can generally be advantageous to have a realistic and straightforward approach towards personal tasks and responsibilities and have a healthy dose of self-confidence and effective strategies for dealing with stress and frustration. It will then be easier to take on a more rational position, stay aware of your personal and professional boundaries, and act calm and assertive. These factors also prevent impulsive reactions directed back towards these kinds of demanding (provocative) people. These reactions can cause escalations when there is no real need for it.

How about the relation to other forms of aggression?

In many cases, demanding behaviour proves to be a gateway to a transition of aggression into other, more intense, invasive and detrimental types. The tension has already reached a higher level than a "normal" state of being, and people have an offensive mindset. These demanding individuals have "something" to lose. At this stage, people already have stopped communicating attentively and respectfully. They aren't considerate towards other people's needs. Even when this kind of aggressive behaviour is somewhat common in daily human reality, its potential to lead to conflict and even trigger an escalation should be kept in mind.

On the positive side, low-intensity and straightforward interventions can still be successfully and efficiently applied. Suppose we would decide to wait to intervene until the dynamics already have reached a higher level of intensity. In that case, we must deal with a much higher level of excitement, hostility, and risk for impulsive (violent) behaviour. I can only recommend acting immediately, without hesitating too long. By doing so, you can restore balance in the relation. It then could be an option to approach this individual in a more supportive or cooperative manner.

Aggressive manipulation

The concept of aggressive manipulation is the influencing of individual decision-making processes and, therefore, behavioural tendencies using external interferences. In most cases, the victim is not consciously aware that he has been affected and manipulated. Manipulations are effective as soon as verbal and nonverbal communicated messages manage to influence another's feelings. These feelings combined with stress eventually trigger emotions causing a change of behaviour. These triggered emotions incapacitate normal capabilities to stay composed, have clear, rational thoughts and reflect on one's actions. Emotions are also known as the "movers". Emotions unify personal feelings, the results of situational assessments and the willingness or readiness to act.

Effective manipulations change the way people behave. This makes it possible for a manipulator to exert power and control his victim. This benefits the satisfying of certain personal needs for the manipulator. A typical example is when an aggressor compensates or edges away subjective treats and anxiousness by manipulating others into becoming scared or losing their composure.

Manipulative actions can also be quite diverse in their invasiveness. They can be very offensive and, therefore, trigger intense emotions and reactions. These kinds of offensive manipulations mainly affect the victim's need for security negatively or, as with provocative offending actions, they have direct impacts on a more personal (ego) level. The ego, however, also has an indirect function in sustaining a feeling of security and keeping an internal balance. The ego is like an outer shell or shield. Making people feel guilty is also an example of a manipulative mechanism that can create insecurity.

Except for the 'not so hard to detect' manipulative forms, which are accompanied by distinct unpleasant feelings and stress, subtle manipulations affecting more positive connoted feelings like raising sympathy or creating physical attraction are distinguished too. These variations in the manipulative spectrum are much more challenging to detect. It is also the question of whether this is relevant in the context of this book and its specific theme, namely "aggression". Manipulating is also a normal phenomenon because we humans constantly influence each other to satisfy our own needs. These "normal" manipulations and efforts to influence each other also make themselves noticeable by the distinct behavioural cues and the content of messages sent out and received during our daily interactions. It can be quite interesting to pay more attention to the general principle of "manipulation" in social relations.

It bears mentioning that providing subjective information in social media or news can be used in a very destructive way as well. This is manipulation on a mental level. This information creates mental models, influencing people's views and behaviour. The principle of manipulations and generally related themes like "heteronomy" and "self-determination" are regularly discussed among social scientists, psychologists and philosophers. These discussions, however, have more of an ethical and moral nature.

For me, to cut it short, the valuation of whether forms of manipulations are to be considered destructive and therefore unwanted or not depends on how people feel affected by them on a personal level.

Some day in the past, the first commercial billboard was erected. People were outraged because of the way they were being influenced by the message on this advertisement board.

Manipulations lead to power and control

Whenever manipulative actions affect somebody, the aggressive manipulator exerts power and control over the victim. Having power over people means they will act according to the expectations of the aggressive manipulator concerning his specific aspirations. The manipulator generates "co-players", so to speak, for a movie he is the director as well as the protagonist oft. Being able to exercise control over other people could have a preventative effect regarding potential discrepancies or, in other words, it usually compensates for and eradicates hypothetical threats. It isn't laborious to imagine it getting continuously difficult and even nearly impossible to comply with certain professional tasks (especially concerning rules, standards, demands, and arrangements) if you are at your workplace and start reacting overly agitated or even become afraid.

The invasiveness of manipulations as a criterion

When we consider that humans constantly influence and affect each other on a personal level and we realise this is a part of our social nature and regarded as standard, a usable criterion is needed that determines if and when manipulations actually can be seen as something unwanted and harmful in social relationships. This criterion depends on the invasiveness, forcefulness, and the extent to which personal needs are being put under pressure or negatively affected, like the need to feel secure. As a result, the valuation of whether manipulations are aggressive or not more or less depends on the perception of the individual affected by it. The actual position, whether victim or observer, is relevant and important. Sometimes a victim is not aware that he is being manipulated, for example, into feeling guilty. An observer could have a completely different estimation regarding the situation. This book orientates itself from the victim's position and not the person "only" observing the interaction.

Due to manipulations and their specific mechanisms, victims will try to preserve or compensate for their negatively affected needs. These so-called "secondary compensatory needs" usually differ from the pre-existing ambitions before a person is manipulated. For example, someone is socialising (social needs) at a party and then, caused by a conflict, suddenly gets intimidated by an aggressive guest. In this instance, a sudden shift in behaviour occurs. It will become more critical to preserve the basic need for security than following the initial ambitions of having a drink since this situation is threatening. This adaption is a result of the security-related feelings being negatively influenced due to intimidating gestures. These responses to hostility and the shifting attention of the victim will result in some way favouring the manipulator.

Regarding the form of aggression by "manipulation of the emotions", some varieties in the action spectrum are to be distinguished. The mechanisms interrelate with the broad spectrum of possible human feelings and emotions. This means that all human feelings can possibly be manipulated with the use of external forces. The typical manipulative forces, however, obviously connoted with aggression and destructive acts are intimidations and provocations. These mechanisms have distinctive, aggressive behavioural characteristics and cause typical aggression-related negative feelings and sensations.

Intimidation and provocation – the usual suspects

Intimidations are effective whenever they cause high stress, anxiousness - the sensation of insecurity and even fear. With both nonverbal and verbal expressions, the intimidator tries to influence their opponent negatively. Intimidations are, in most cases, overt offensive acts. The distinct behavioural characteristics are extremely threatening to most people. However, the degree to which people feel threatened depends on the individual being targeted. This has to do with differences in dispositions like experiences, individual sensibility and resilience. As a result of effective intimidation, the victim will try to compensate, for example, by an actual physical withdrawal. Some people are even going to suffer from a kind of paralysis due to a stress reaction. Victims could also act submissively. Responses like these basically indicate that intimidation has had its effect.

It should always be kept in mind that this form of aggression could rapidly shift. The acting out of frustrations and even intentional violence are real possibilities. These forms are more dangerous. It is important to remain alert and watchful and consider if it is worth actively balancing out this aggressive behaviour. It is further important to keep a safe physical distance to prevent sudden violent physical attacks and always keep an exit available. Attempts of physical violence cannot be averted effectively with instinctive protective reactions if you allow aggressive people to come too close. There will barely be any time and space to (unconsciously) detect an attack and successfully defend against it through instincts and reflexes.

Attempting to set boundaries while being insecure generally isn't a good idea. Most intimidating individuals will get more aggressive. This can easily lead to a total escalation of the situation. The impact on a psychological level is much larger when feeling overwhelmed, powerless and at the mercy of the aggressor in case of an escalation. I have often experienced these effects in my profession.

Provocations differ from intimidations in many ways. The word itself comes from the Latin verb "Provocare", which means to evoke, test, or challenge. The principle of provocations is to cause an internal conflict by influencing another person negatively on an ego level with offensive actions. These impacts induce agitation, frustration, and may even provoke impulsive, offensive behaviour and a violent act on behalf of the victim. As a result, the aggressor can now directly or indirectly satisfy his personal needs. Provocations can be very subtle, and provocative messages sometimes are transmitted without the recipient even being able to perceive them on a conscious level. Yet, on most occasions, it will manifest itself in a very overtly offensive way. Still, even then, the main characteristics of provocative behaviour are generally less distinctly offensive than aggressive intimidations.

An effective provocation addresses invasive messages towards personal boundaries represented by a self-securing mechanism known as the "ego". Mainly, the victim's overcompensated, and latent feelings of low self-confidence and low self-esteem could be targeted by deliberately scratching and poking this outer shell. Provocative attacks usually are not entirely forced through, as would be the case with intimidations. Offensive insults and verbal assaults are often followed by nonverbal gestures (averting the eyes), suggesting a kind of withdrawal. This combination of "attack" and "withdrawal" makes it even harder for the victim to resist provocations and to not react offensively or at least defensively. Provocations can have many functions. Like with intimidations, a general goal is to control a situation and to exert power.

Some examples of motivations leading to provocative behaviour:

> ➤ A relationship can be tested by provoking a certain resonance from an opposite person. This is common amongst children and teens and a part of their normal development processes. They test boundaries and basically where they are at in social relations.
> ➤ With provocations, it is possible to "soften up" rigid personal boundaries. It can be used to get in contact with someone by triggering a minor conflict. An opening is formed, and this makes it possible to connect and build a relationship.
> ➤ Provocations could evoke a defensive reaction and lead to actual fights. Some provocative people use these defensive reactions of their victims to justify acting violent. These fights can be used to boost their self-esteem and makes them feel better about themselves in some perverted way.
> ➤ The reactions of the victim to a provocation and the conflict it causes can be used by the provoker as a reason to let off tension and feelings of frustration.
> ➤ It is possible to draw attention in favour of your own concerns.
> ➤ Having power over other people can also directly satisfy needs. For example, it is sadistically enjoyed when other people get very upset internally but still must behave professionally and control themselves at all costs. In some professions (social institutions, customer support), people feel they cannot act assertively towards aggression because of the social context and the belief (or social delusion) that it is "not done". Some do not know how to act assertively to balance out aggressive behaviour. They assume it is expected to remain sort of cooperative, supportive and overly polite at all times. This can create feelings of helplessness and powerlessness. The aggression is, therefore, "absorbed" and creates stress and massive impressions.
> ➤ Provocations can also directly satisfy needs, for example, when employees lose their self-control causing impulsive and emotional responses. As a result, they are not able to keep a clear mind and to act professionally. This can create opportunistic chances for the aggressor.

To deal with provocations effectively, balance out the dynamics, and de-escalate the situation, it is necessary to stay calm and control one's stress reactions and feelings of frustration. It is important not to fulfil the projected expectations of the aggressor and to remain constantly aware of and set your personal boundaries. Usually, individuals who are not likely to feel insulted or are not easily upset are less likely to become victims of this kind of aggression. Manipulations are always a result of a combination of the aggressor and the victim. The effects that aggressive provocations have on us tell us a lot about ourselves. Due to the nature of aggressive mechanisms, personal attributes and subconscious vulnerabilities are being addressed and exposed.

Aggressive acts out of frustration

The word frustration comes from the Latin "Frustratio". It means the disappointment of an expectation. The feeling of frustration is often a result of multiple failing efforts to satisfy one's personal needs but is also caused by adverse external influences and impacts. Frustrating experiences often cumulate, and the distinct accompanying negative feelings increase progressively with every new actual disappointment. Even personal subjective perceptions of experiences and phantasies and imaginations of frustrating occurrences can cause this to happen.

This progressive build-up of negative tension caused by frustrating experiences is likely to occur. We all are more or less familiar with this phenomenon. It is not always possible to immediately find a compensating need or to act assertively to compensate for frustration. If no compensations are found, or stress isn't let off by any other means, this ongoing process eventually leads to a massive build-up and congestion of physical tension. Negative feelings caused by frustration will increase too, like anxiousness (as one feels exposed), sadness and helplessness (because of the impression that it is impossible to change this situation accordingly and one feels at the mercy of external forces) and anger.

Control mechanisms eventually fail when the internal pressure further increases past a certain ability to suppress and control this build-up of internal pressure. At some point, it will be impossible to control oneself any further. The slightest conflict can lead to impulsive, potentially dangerous, and unpredictable actions and the destruction of material objects. It is not hard to imagine that it would be principally better to somehow look for opportunities to decrease one's internal pressure by finding alternative ways to let off one's anger and therefore preventing this kind of aggression.

46

Venting pent-up emotions and stress principally leads to a so-called catharsis. However, this isn't always possible, and most often, it is perceived as being inappropriate. Also, we are commonly taught how to control ourselves and not show our emotions, but we are seldom taught how to deal with negative feelings and stress. We are used to it high levels of stress nowadays and control our pent-up emotions effectively. This altogether is responsible for causing explosive emotional reactions I call "aggression out of frustration".

This venting utilising high energetic and impulsive behaviour to release tension is a way to regain an energetic and emotional balance and rational perspective. This relief of built-up tension can be seen as a human need. Maintaining a high level of physical arousal is an unhealthy alternative. It eventually leads to all kinds of psychological and physical discomforts and diseases. This is well known in relation to chronic stress. Venting pent-up emotions is an (unconscious) destructive strategy to achieve this cleansing and internal pressure releasing effect. This behaviour inflicts negative impacts on other people. It generally causes massive stress due to the uncertainty it creates. Especially when personal (physical) boundaries are being crossed. However, this meaning of this behaviour is the venting of built-up energy and the expression of feelings of powerlessness, hopelessness, anger and fear. It is not aggression on a personal level. This is a big difference even when we feel personally negatively affected by it. Aggression out of frustration can also become personal and potentially **lead to** violence, and this is a fact. However, we need to concentrate on the challenges in the present. We should try not to act upon problems that are not there in reality and based on presumptions. This isn't easy under the influence of stress, but with training and experience, it becomes easier.

How do we normally deal with feelings of frustration?

We all know to some extent how it feels to be frustrated. Frustration can occur if we are incapable of satisfying our own needs or if we feel negatively affected by others or by the actions of some organisation, like an institution or government. Distractions and substituting needs mostly compensate for our negative experiences and disappointments. These help to balance out the adverse effects of frustration. The physical excitement itself could also be reduced and compensated by activities. A good example of this principle is the release of frustration by doing all kinds of sports, using relaxation techniques like yoga and meditation, or by distracting oneself and concentrating on other themes. However, disappointments are mostly not completely substituted by these alternatives. These activities only reduce tension and restore balance temporarily. Those frustrated needs may stay relevant for an individual on a subconscious level. It can be a matter of time until these initial aspirations re-emerge in social interactions, with sometimes more or less the same challenges for all involved depending on what caused these strivings to fail in the first place. Some needs just cannot be fulfilled.

A general advantage of reducing tension due to stress-reducing activities is that it will help in being able to think clearly again and find solutions. It also reduces the risk of tense mental fixations considering perceived ambitions. Fixations in thinking processes could lead to dark, hateful thoughts, projected hostility, negative transferences, mental blockages and resistances. This also implies that the openness for alternatives and the ability to put things into perspective are progressively lost as soon as people become more fixated and obsessed. These effects of fixations could end up having negative consequences and occasionally cause complicated interactions between people.

Some people are not able to adapt and to find alternatives or restore inner balance in the event of frustrating experiences. However, this internal pressure must be reduced eventually. Control over negative feelings and internal pressure, as described earlier, cannot be achieved permanently. At some point, depending on individual control mechanisms, the height of the level of tension and the meaning of social interactions mostly being beyond our control, an uncontrolled outburst of emotions can take place.

Aggressive acts done out of frustration are explosive by nature. This form of aggression cannot (and often should not) easily be controlled by talking and asking people to calm down. These reactions sometimes occur instantly as soon as people feel disappointed, especially when the affected needs are of importance. This acting out can also happen later, representing a more "suitable" occasion for the frustrated individual. This depends on the person and the context he finds himself in. How often have you been confronted with people acting out, frustrated at the slightest conflict, and you did not have a clue how this could happen?

Children and teens tend to show their feelings immediately when they are frustrated. Adults tend to regulate, control and suppress their emotions more effectively. Mostly they were taught as children to do so ("Behave yourself!"), and it is still a general belief that people always have to keep themselves composed. This attitude, however, ultimately is going to lead to much stronger and potentially even more dangerous behaviour. A massive accumulation of negative thoughts, feelings, and stress can cause sudden, destructive actions and turn people violent.

Typical behaviour

Before people start to act out aggressively, some specific tell-tale and distinctive preliminary behavioural cues can be observed:

- ➢ withdrawal from everyday social interactions
- ➢ turning inwardly
- ➢ increased muscular tension
- ➢ speaking in short sentences
- ➢ general restlessness
- ➢ the (subtle) defamation of other people
- ➢ defensive behaviour

In the eventuality that people lose their self-control, they shout furiously out of helplessness and anger while sometimes damaging property. Some also launch a physical attack like grabbing clothes and slapping another person or pushing, hitting and kicking. Because of these explosive outbursts of emotions and the threatening nature of such actions, they automatically trigger a stress reaction and can cause a (temporary) inability to deal with the situation adequately. It is likely to overwhelm us and make us feel instantly helpless and powerless. A mental overload is mainly caused because people were not prepared. Due to lack of experience or distractions of all sorts, preliminary warning signs can remain unnoticed or sometimes they are ignored. Stress reactions are triggered too because people instantly presume violence is imminent and inevitable. And indeed, in the event people start acting out, all possibilities are open. A threat of a physical attack is imminent when people completely lose control over their internal impulses. This can happen, for example, when people attempt to control and actively influence this highly agitated and emotionally unstable person by trying to calm him down, keep on talking, and making physical contact. It is likely that the tension will get too high and the emotions too strong if this person is put under additional (verbal) pressure. Anger and even rage could instantly be directed outwards, and it is possible that interfering people, possibly instinctively being perceived as a threat, are going to be (mis-)used as a physical "lightning rod": They might be on the receiving end of a reflexive, defensive punch or slap in the face. However, for me, there is still a fundamental difference between, on the one hand, this impulsive, defensive violence, and on the other hand, deliberate physical violence. I will describe this difference later in more detail.

Until somebody completely loses his self-control, they somehow manage to control their actions, even if it might seem different from the observing point of view. The control mechanisms remain to some degree sufficient and prevent real catastrophic situations from occurring. This frustrating acting out will mostly be limited to verbal aggression. If property gets damaged, it is mainly going to affect objects that will not cause physical injuries. Moreover, you will frequently find that the destroyed or damaged objects do not represent too much sentimental or material value. I often observed that the damaged things were somehow representative, for instance, responsible for frustrating this person in the first place, like caretakers.

As I mentioned before, physical violence is always a realistic possibility when people completely lose their self-control. The level of stress of these people is very high, and the emotions are unstable. It is sometimes impossible to tell what is happening within people by observing them, as distinct warning signs or behavioural cues are not always noticeable. In case you want to intervene, always consider this fact for your safety. A sudden transition into deliberate physical violence without any prior warning could also occur, making things even more dangerous. Remind yourself of the following basic rules: be careful with any further demands and always keep an adequate distance. Abiding by these basic rules generally prevents getting physically attacked, but equally importantly, you will have the opportunity to react and defend yourself by instinct in case it happens. With an arm's length distance, preliminary signs of an imminent physical attack can usually be perceived before it happens. Being confronted with sudden physical violent attacks is almost always a result of disregarding the basic rules for maintaining security, lacking attention for and ignoring preliminary warning signs and accepting that people are unpredictable by nature.

Intentional physical violence

The main characteristic of this form of aggression is pursuing personal goals by using physical or psychological violence. These goals could be deflecting actual or perceived danger, raising self-worth, forcing someone to abandon a certain (professional) position or satisfying diverse personal needs like experiencing power or security by suppressing and degrading victims. This form of aggression is the most invasive, harmful, and potentially most dangerous of all. Intentional violent people are full of hate, focused and/or lack any form of empathy and attention to other peoples' integrity. To put this kind of violent behaviour under control requires a lot of effort and energetic resources. At the same time, a real risk of being hurt by a physical attack is more imminent than ever. Often intentional physical and psychological violence no sooner ceases until its goal has been achieved and, therefore, its purpose has been fulfilled. The confrontation with people willing to use physical violence upon you releases an automatic fight-or-flight response to keep you out of harm's way. Some professions (i.e., the police) learned how to control and restrain a violent person and re-establish basic safety.

Intentional physical violence such as kicking, hitting, strangling, sexual attacks and weapons use can cause serious injuries, including even death: it further will have massive psychological impacts on victims. These deliberate attacks can occur out of pure impulse (hate), and sometimes, however less commonly, they are being consciously planned and executed deliberately. Typically for this form of aggression, a mental picture of the attack being executed is more (planned action) or less (impulsive act out of blind rage and hate) formed before it takes place. This is also why the main characteristics of intentional violent aggression are described as focused, powerful and determined, and the effects for the victim can therefore turn out to be devastating.

This is in contrast to an impulsive, defensive kick, hit or slap done out of frustration. This kind of violence also has the potential to leave severe injuries and is no less dangerous. However, these attacks lack focus and attention and are uncontrolled and chaotic by nature. An impulsive physical attack is mainly triggered whenever people actively act upon (grabbing hold, touching), for example, a highly frustrated person.

These people strike out and hit or kick out of reflex. Perceived from the aggressor's perspective, this physical violence is then a defensive reaction to pressure exerted by people trying to interfere (or intervene).

To determine whether an attack is impulsive and defensive or deliberate is never going to be easy, especially when you are in the midst of it all. I solely make this distinction to describe the difference and point out that impulsive physical reactions are more common than deliberate violent attacks. People deliberately using violence have a completely different mindset. Impulsive attacks can be prevented by adapting and respecting the potential danger and being aware that somebody might feel (subjectively) threatened if we acted upon this individual, even when it is done out of the best of intentions.

It is much more challenging to prevent deliberate attacks. Intentional violence can occur even if you are utterly oblivious of the danger at hand and without having any relation with the attacker. There is not much you can do in the event you are being perceived as a hate object or you are in the way of a person willing to use offensive physical violence as he sees fit, except for defending yourself or getting into safety. Also, the processes leading to this kind of dangerous behaviour take place in the mind of this other person. These processes are inaccessible to outsiders and are hard or even impossible to influence and control. I do not recommend any experimenting. Instead, always choose to protect your safety first and always keep an adequate distance from any perceived threat.

Another aspect of this form of aggression is that besides the physical injuries, this kind of deliberate violence cause psycho-emotional impacts and trauma. The problem with these impacts on a psycho-emotional level or traumas is the difficulty distinguishing them or, in case people compensate for them very well, they will show hardly any observable signs. Also, a victim who is not aware of the seriousness of psychological trauma is unlikely to consider this aspect and will usually resume his activities and behave like business as usual. These adverse effects take more time and are more complicated to heal than most physical injuries. Traumas can be processed and integrated, but they could also persist for years and years and have devastating implications on the lives of victims as post-traumatic stress disorders.

Realistic verbal threats to use violence can be distinguished from pure intimidation. Both will cause stress, insecurity and fear. However, if somebody expresses the willingness to use violent force upon you, like in the sense of a kind of promise no one asked for, this will have a more profound impact. These kinds of messages are typically brought in a controlled fashion and are heavily charged and unambiguous. As I said, it is more like a promise of what will happen if the demands are not being met. To act with physical violence is a realistic option for this individual. He already has made up his mind.

Intimidations are verbal threats that are being expressed to manipulate a victim on an emotional level. With manipulations, the main goal is to exercise power and control and compensate for possible frustration in advance. However, it should never be forgotten that manipulations could also transform into physical violence in case the aggressor gets frustrated or when you do not behave according to his expectations. In summary, there are distinctive differences between pure intimidations on an emotional level and clear "promises" of violent actions or repercussions. Concerning this matter, it is also difficult to distinguish between both, especially on acute stressful occasions. Only with training, experience, and real-life confrontations can one make out the difference in these kinds of borderline dangerous situations.

Forms of aggression can change as the dynamics develop.

I separately described the forms of aggression: demanding behaviour, aggressive manipulations, acts out of frustration and intentional physical violence. During the progression of the dynamics, you could be confronted with different forms. These shifts can take place very quickly and suddenly. In most situations, especially when you have recurring experiences with the aggression of certain individuals, you will be able to observe repeating behavioural patterns. This fact makes it predictable what can be expected, but it will not provide a 100% guarantee of what will happen. Acts of aggression could suddenly change and alternate. This should always be kept in mind. Taking caution is important, even if you are dealing with the same difficult person all over again. Complacency considering your estimations of the situation and considering adapting your attitude, could get you into trouble quickly. Complacency kills, they used to say in the army.

Every form of aggression demands a different approach to be successful in de-escalating or keeping you safe. Normally, your strategy has to change as the dynamics take their course. This will put us under even more pressure. Anyway, we will have no other choice than to "go with the flow" and compose ourselves if we want to be effective and keep ourselves out of harm's way at the same time. Every individual has capabilities and personal limitations to deal with difficult and sometimes dangerous situations. Because an instinctive stress reaction is likely to take over if forms of aggression shift, we will probably lose our self-control and act impulsively. This shifting makes aggressive mechanisms become even more effective in reaching a certain (unconscious) goal. But also, the risk factor and danger level will often increase whenever our instincts and emotions are taking over.

It is a difficult task to be on top of these kinds of highly tense interactions, stay composed, be able to differentiate (intuitively) between the various meanings effectively and act accordingly. Of fundamental importance towards coping with these challenging situations is having actual practical experience dealing with these kinds of people, strategies to manage emerging stress reactions, having some sound common sense, and knowing when to leave if things get too dangerous.

Step 2: Distinguish the form of aggression

After successfully controlling yourself by breathing techniques or one of the other principles I explained, (intuitively) identifying the predominant form of aggression is the next step.

Intentional physical violence

Sometimes there is no time to assess a situation calmly. Physical attacks can occur suddenly, for instance, if somebody loses self-control and turns violent. Still, suppose you would find yourself being confronted with an individual ready to use physical violence. In that case, you could observe the following typical behavioural cues and physical warning signs: cold, piercing eyes, a frosty stare, acting calm and reserved, keyed up but having controlled behaviour, an overall offensive, but still composed attitude, a dominant, decisive, overly bold and self-confident posture.

If you are dealing with a highly frustrated or provocative person, you may also observe all kinds of tell-tale indications for imminent, intentional physical violence. Then you will start to become aware that it is you who is being seen and sized up as a direct target. The look in the eyes of somebody shortly before attacking you grows darker and more penetrating. This focusing of attention prepares him mentally and therefore physically to direct his violent aggression onto you. You can also observe the decreasing of chaotic behaviour that usually is brought in relation to aggression. As a result, the pressure resulting from this dangerous situation can be felt, and stress will rise very high. This is a natural reaction because instincts prepare your system to react by flight-or-fight in case of an attack.

Most people confronted with aggressors who threaten them with physical violence immediately experience enormous internal pressure. Most become locked up in fear, get into a state of shock and are petrified. At the very least, confrontation makes people feel very uncomfortable. Some even feel a sensation of inner cold, and they do not know what to say or do. Individuals prepared to use violence to enforce their demands often show overly self-conscious, highly self-confident, dominant, calculating and fearless characteristics. Dealing with this is a terrifying experience. These individuals will also often show absolutely no signs of empathy and concerns regarding the implications these actions might have on others.

In the event an actual direct physical attack is launched, instinctive mechanisms will trigger a stress reaction. Adrenalin is released and primitive effects that should keep you safe and enable a flight-or-fight reaction kick in. Some people also wholly freeze, as if extracting themselves from the outside world and curling up into an embryonic state. They are unable to move. Other affected individuals stay active but end up behaving very chaotically. Not all people can withdraw from a dangerous situation in a controlled way or even manage to fight to ward off hazardous situations without at some point losing their self-control. The main unconscious goal for most people is to relatively improve the dangerous unfavourable circumstances with all means available. What you will see are people reacting extremely chaotically and impulsively. Mostly only trained, experienced professionals react to physical violence by applying effective self-defensive measures and using controlling and restraining techniques to stay safe. They acquired the experience and gathered the necessary skills by extensive training and repeatedly practising drills.

The outcome of these kinds of dangerous situations with violent people will largely depend on the kind of violent force used upon you, the type of individual who uses it against you, and your capabilities to apply defensive countermeasures. It also remains difficult to predict how one will react when put in such a high-stress situation. However, you can be sure that this confrontation with directed physical violence used against you will be an experience that will push you to your limits, no matter how experienced and skilled you are. Training can help to apply defensive techniques, remain safe or escape in a controlled manner. I would never advise people to get into a fight with any aggressive person who uses physical violent force upon them without showing any signs of hesitation. This does not provide any safety; either you win or lose a battle. It is as simple as that. The best thing is to defend yourself and ward off such attacks for as long as necessary and then withdraw as soon as possible. Adapting to the situation is better than fighting it.

I am regularly asked what the law dictates regarding applying self-defensive techniques and meet people who assume they have the right to respond to attacks by using excessive force. Suppose you "decide" to use self-defensive techniques to compensate for physical violence. In that case, you should be aware of this fact: the defensive measures you apply will be assessed by the Department of Justice according to the rules of law applicable in your country. These laws can differ quite a lot from country to country. However, in most countries, there must be a balance between the type of violent force being used upon you and, therefore, the danger level and the applied defensive countermeasures. Using excessive counterforce could lead to legal problems.

Aggressive acts out of frustration

The characteristics of this form of aggression are very distinctive. Most people get caught by surprise by the sudden outburst of rage and anger accompanying this form of aggression. Sometimes only the slightest conflict can cause the control mechanisms to fail. Perceived from the "outside", we tend to say: "This person lost his temper"; "He burst out in rage"; or "He is acting out".

Aggressive acts of frustration are accompanied by very high levels of excitement and emotional instability. Highly frustrated people scream, shout, act offensively and hostile, and become verbally abusive. They sometimes even turn violent. This could also lead to the damaging of property. A real risk of impulsive physical attacks by punches, slaps and kicks is always imminent and must be considered. When somebody is acting out emotionally, their actions show no direction. This behaviour resembles a needle in a compass not being able to find its true north, and therefore it keeps spinning around unpredictably. This acting out corresponds with this person's shifting feelings and emotions, like anxiousness, fear, anger, helplessness, powerlessness, sadness and rage. Acting out or venting frustration has a kind of cleansing effect for the person. Nevertheless, this form of aggression is likely to be accompanied by intrusive actions such as offensive manipulations. People will then use this other form of aggression to try to influence the situation in their favour and to regain control after the initial strivings failed, in an attempt to ward off the sometimes inevitable, which is experiencing frustration.

It is generally important and helpful (I think) not to take pure frustrated behaviour and these emotional outbursts too personally. As long as you manage to stay centred, grounded, and guard yourself by raising a "mental shield" to deflect these energetic outbursts, you will generally feel less affected. I can tell because I use these passive, mental self-defensive principles regularly as I encounter a lot of confrontations with this kind of aggression. It is a structural part of my profession. I seldom experienced people actually becoming dangerous, except for situations that weren't appropriately assessed, to begin with, and co-workers made it dangerous by acting inadequately. It is not effortless to keep a clear mind and to stay focused while dealing with these kinds of situations, but this is an important goal you should keep in mind. Except for not taking it too personally and mentally guarding yourself, it is also of vital importance to always stay aware of your physical safety and, for example, by keeping a safe distance or even to withdraw from the situation in an orderly fashion if it gets too dangerous from your own observation (or from somebody else's observation who informs you that it would be better to leave).

As long as a stress reaction and feelings of frustration do not overwhelm you and lead to impulsive reactions on your behalf, a feeling of helplessness and powerlessness can be sensed in most cases. These familiar sensations emerge because there often won't be many opportunities to actively help a highly frustrated person calm down and, therefore, influence and control this behaviour. This results from high levels of excitement, emotional instability, and the loss of cognitive capabilities. Highly agitated people are not able to process communicated messages as they would normally. People typically feel helpless whenever a situation cannot be influenced and because there is no active role to play at one's disposal. This usually means a frustrated person "has to" sort it out and calm down by himself regarding this specific form of aggression.

Then the only thing you could do or the only task that remains is to stay calm or even to withdraw if a frustrated person would get even more agitated because of your presence. It all depends on the relation to the person and the circumstances. What you always can and should do, however, is to remain "switched on" and to follow the basic rules like getting some backup help, keeping an arm's length distance, looking for a quick, available exit and, very importantly, observing the development of the changing dynamics acutely. Depending on the (professional) context, the main goal is to prevent the (massive) damaging of property and other dangerous actions which could require (depending on the professional context) immediate actions to re-establish the safety for those involved and affected.

Frustrated people occasionally transmit various messages while acting out, and they could also subtly express a need for help and support. We then can feel empathy and compassion for this person. These subtle messages are sometimes concretely verbalised, but primarily they are being transmitted "in between the lines" by minimalistic suggestions (expressions of helplessness, a "questioning look" in the eyes) and other transferences. Before acting or talking should even be considered, it is important that this aggressive person is "asking" for aid. The desire from a lot of people to influence and control a straining situation should not be mistaken for the possible need that a frustrated person might have to be supported to manage his crisis. Most people find it hard to remain calm, to just observe and to stay passive. However, it is essential to control yourself and to be thoughtful regarding any possible interventions. With frustration, the pressure is already very high, the emotions are likely to be unstable and impulsive reactions are easily triggered. An escalation could create a dangerous situation very quickly. Sometimes it is just required to deal with your own feelings of helplessness and powerlessness and be aware of what these sensations indicate concerning your circumstances. It will be probably better to wait, stay calm, endure, and have patience for an opportune moment to come. Then it is more likely you are going to be effective in de-escalating the situation.

Staying in control of your emotions is not an easy task. I often experience that out of feelings of helplessness and powerlessness, the sensation of frustration and angry feelings quickly arise. As you might know from your own experiences, you will probably proceed according to these negative feelings, even when the initial motivation for your actions seems to be coming from the best intentions. In many cases, my co-workers were physically attacked when they (re-) acted too soon, got too close and even made physical contact because they lost their composure. Frustrated persons can be pushed over the edge quite easily, getting violent as soon as you put them under additional pressure and/or your actions are subjectively perceived as threatening intrusions. A (defensive) kick to the legs or a punch to the face, even when conducted impulsively and in an uncontrolled way, nevertheless could induce serious injuries.

Also, in the case where people initially show this form of aggression, it is possible that at some moment, they are going to use directed physical violence to achieve their goals and punch, hit and kick with better aim. Whenever a situation matures more face-to-face, note that this could be an important indication for imminent physical violence with intent to cause significant harm to you. Signs indicating that this furious person is getting more focused on you are a penetrating look in his eyes and an increasing fear and stress level within you.

You are now being sized up. Probably you (in your professional role) are being hated and a potential direct target. In general, the most important thing is always to remain aware of your safety. This fundamental principle always has top priority.

Aggressive manipulation: provocation and intimidation

The main difference between aggressive manipulations and the characteristics of people acting aggressively out of frustration is the quality of verbal and nonverbal communication. When people try to manipulate aggressively, the goal is to intentionally influence the feelings of a victim negatively. A manipulator can also be distinguished from a person threatening and promising to use violent force intentionally if his demands aren't being met. A manipulator tries to influence an opponent with his aggressive actions to reach his goal, and, therefore, your feelings are the main target of his actions. Manipulations are not as cold-hearted and self-orientated in comparison to individuals willing to use deliberate physical aggression onto other people. On the contrary, manipulative actions use instinctive human mechanisms or even known individual "weak spots" of a familiar victim in a deliberate opportunistic way. These vulnerabilities are related to the victim's personality traits and get instinctively sized up by the aggressor. The manipulative effects lead to a shift in perception of the situation by the victim. This will change his behaviour, for example, towards being scared or angry. Distinct aggressive signals trigger instinctive mechanisms within all people. For subtle and more effective manipulations, it is an advantage to know the victim personally. If people act aggressively merely out of built-up frustration, you most likely will also feel affected on an emotional level, but these actions are not deliberately used to manipulate. This acting out has an entirely different function, even if it might seem just as threatening to some people. This is because the verbal and nonverbal signals have more or less the same characteristics and fit the same general pattern of aggression.

Being intimidated

The excitement of an overtly intimidating individual is semi-high to high compared to other forms of aggression. The nonverbal and verbal messages are offensive, threatening, hostile and personal boundaries are crossed. These behavioural characteristics cause the typical intimidating effect. Based on the type of intimidation and its implication on your sense of security, you will start to feel anxious, afraid and could even experience real fear. The general goals of manipulations are to exert power and to control the targeted person. This satisfies all kinds of personal needs for the intimidating aggressor, like getting a better position in a waiting queue or securing a bargain deal. A conflict could also easily be the reason for intimidating others. It then compensates for experiencing uncertainty and anxiety for the aggressor. By experiencing power and control, a subjective feeling of security is being maintained. If you are being personally affected, it is difficult to realise that avoiding anxiety motivates this aggressive behaviour. But as the famous psychoanalytic Eric Fromm described: "The basic motivator for behaviour in social relations is the avoidance of experiencing anxiety".

Being provoked

Provocations are similar to intimidations. The main difference, though, is that with provocation, the qualities of the expressed messages are less invasive and offensive than intimidations. Additionally, the motivation for this form of aggression is slightly different. Tell-tale signs of provocation are people deliberately offending and insulting others. Provocation orientates itself around personal boundaries. These representations of the self are being negatively affected by insulting, offending messages. A provocation based on a rapid "attack and withdrawal combination is quite common and very effective. This means that after the verbal insulting or offending, the provocateur turns his body away from the victim or looks away and interrupts the initial eye contact. Most affected people instinctively react to provocation in an emotional, angry and hostile way. This is what causes the manipulative effect, generally known as "being provoked". The emotional reaction caused by provocation provides manipulative individuals with the control they are unconsciously looking for and enables them to exert power over the general situation and the victims involved. Indirectly, this control and power lead to the satisfaction of personal needs, similar to the principle of intimidation. If provocative people try to pick a fight by provoking hostile reactions, this form of aggression could even lead to the instant satisfaction of their own personal needs. "Who is the stronger one of us both?", is an example of this. Provocations can be very subtle if insulting messages are transmitted implicitly and "in between the lines". However, these subtle, provocative messages are just as well likely to trigger extreme defensive reactions.

In case you are not personally affected and only observing such a situation, it will be hard to tell from the outside "what it was all about" and what triggered this massive conflict and negative turbulent dynamics in the first place.

Demanding behaviour

This form of aggression can be well recognised, even if its mechanisms are not always that obvious compared to the other types I described earlier. Demanding behaviour causes typical feelings and emotions we are all familiar with but not always that aware of. The tension level of demanding individuals is higher in comparison to them being in a "normal", balanced state of mind. In this stage, people are stressed and agitated. Also, the distinct nonverbal and verbal messages indicate that someone is more offensive and less empathetic. When applying pressure onto others by repeatedly uttering their demands, the people create stress to those affected by this behaviour. In this situation, it is also likely demanding people start crossing lines into others' intimate zones, and by doing so, they exert even more pressure. The main goal of this behaviour is generally to force others to cooperate. Except for causing stress, this is at some point going to lead to frustration for the potential victims. First of all, victims are faced with this enormous pressure, and secondly, the "cornering effect" of this offensive behaviour will have negative consequences concerning personal needs. A typical example of offensive demanding behaviour is the constant concrete or implicit repeating verbal and nonverbal expression of an egoistic desire to have needs satisfied like: "I want, I want, I want!"

Summary

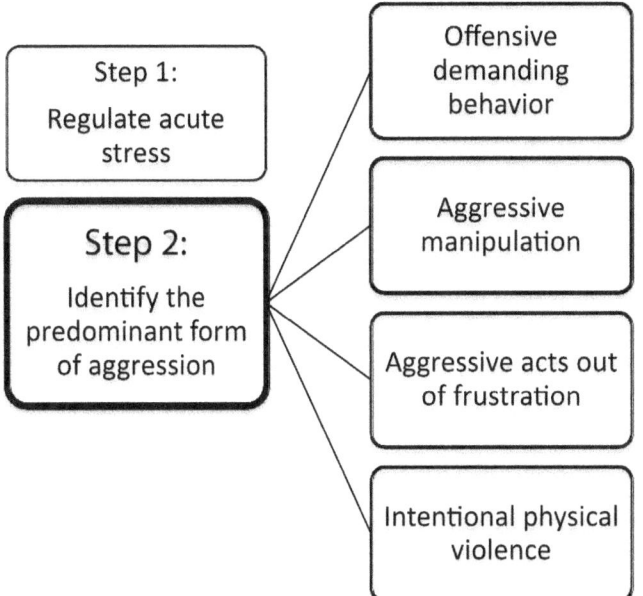

Exercise four: distinguishing forms of aggression

This exercise is based on the first, in which you were asked to describe situations and encounters with "aggressive" people or situations that made you feel anxious, under pressure and uncomfortable. Now you can either combine this exercise with the first one or only go to this specific exercise. The task here is to describe your feelings and internal sensations (for example, stress, anxiousness, anger, fear), concrete observations of behavioural characteristics and your personal assessment regarding forms of aggression you may encounter.

General description of a situation:
What kind of feelings or internal sensations did this cause?
Observed behavioural characteristics of the aggressor:
Matching form of aggression:

*Additional exercise templates can be found on page 138

The next step

After you have managed to distinguish the form of aggression consciously or intuitively, the next step is to adapt your attitude to influence the aggression and keep you safe when it gets too dangerous. An implicit goal will also be to get on eye level to find a constructive solution for the conflict. The way we act upon conflict and aggression can be differentiated into four types of attitudes. These different qualities of attitude have various related positive attributes and can have adverse effects depending on the situation and the kind of interaction. People commonly tend to show some kind of dominant attitude. These are related to the personality of an individual. It characterises this person and the given circumstances. People's attitude generally tends to shift according to their context and its meaning to them.

The great challenge is that when considering dealing with aggression, we cannot limit ourselves to our own attitude we might, for some reason, predominantly tend to gravitate towards. Expecting that our tendencies will provide us with all the positive, constructive and securing effects we need to protect us from aggressive behaviour is unrealistic. Reality shows us that a certain quality of attitude may be effective in dealing with some forms of aggression, but when applied to influence other forms, its features can also cause situations to escalate and become quite dangerous. The conclusion is that it is generally important to be aware of the different qualities, intrinsic values and potencies considering qualities of attitudes.

Several studies about interactions and dynamics between people have clearly differentiated the qualities of attitudes and related effects on interactions in social relations. Especially when working with people daily, it is advisable to "dip" into this material and self-reflect about what kind of attitude you tend to show and how your attitude shifts as soon as situations change. It is to your advantage to be aware of your capabilities and their different attitudes' variable effects on interpersonal interactions. This includes offensive and defensive attitudes, commonly connoted and wrongfully or generalised as "aggressive" and negative. Remind yourself to be flexible and to adjust and adapt in various situations when facing aggressive people. This general mindset enables the effective adjustment for aggressive behaviour and is going to prevent escalations from happening.

3. Mental attitude, de-escalating and resolving of conflict.

In social relations, people can interact with four qualities of mental attitude: offensive, defensive, leading supportive and going along/cooperative. This mental attitude is a product of how we mostly subconsciously evaluate an individual or behaviour of others or a situation in general. This valuation makes itself implicitly noticeable by expressed opinions, our personal feelings and thoughts and the way we behave (act and react), for example, towards people. In the case of conflict and aggression, our mental attitude and, therefore, our reactions depend on our personality, and life experiences with this kind of behaviour and sometimes, in case of real danger, our instincts. The general valuation of situations and behaviour of other people is related to the meaning it has according to one's personal perspective. These qualities have been formed by past experiences and learning processes, and some are deeply rooted. This personal meaning represents the specific needs relevant to an individual under certain given circumstances.

Fundamentally, we all show a predominant quality of attitude depending on the situation we are in. This mental attitude determines how we behave and communicate with others. The communication spectrum consists of concrete verbal messages. These expressed phrases contain a specific meaning for ourselves and the opposite person. However, the meaning of verbal messages is also shaped by the intonation with which the messages are being spoken. Except for verbally expressed messages, nonverbal messages (mimic, gesticulation) and even "vibes" are sent out. Verbally and nonverbally communicated messages are interpreted by receivers. These people will respond individually according to their own (subjective) evaluation and perception of the messages they were affected by. This communication and mutual influence are an ongoing dialectic process, as long as these relations and interactions last.

The subject matter "mental attitude" itself, as described here, is of great value. The position taken in interpersonal interactions according to the assessment of various types of aggression could lead to de-escalation and the resolving of conflict but also escalation and violence. Your reactions with your mental attitude in conflict situations and regarding aggressive people is for a large part going to determine the development outcome of these interactions. During my professional career, I experienced the negative and positive effects from combinations of "forms of aggression" and "qualities of attitude" hands-

66

on on numerous occasions. This ultimately led to my conclusions, whether specific combinations are effective or counterproductive. This chapter is built on this simple but fundamental and essential premise.

In this chapter, I will describe the four primary or central mental attitudes in social interactions. They can become apparent as the structural characteristics of an individual or as a result of situational adaption, for example, if confronted with social challenges. These attitudes all have advantageous or disadvantageous attributes and potencies considering dealing with aggressive dynamics and conflict.

The four basic qualities of attitudes in social interactions are:

➢ Leading, supportive (or rational) attitude
➢ Defensive attitude
➢ Cooperative attitude
➢ Offensive attitude

Leading and supportive (or rational) attitude

The attributes of this mental attitude consist of rational, supportive and directing behavioural qualities. They enable us to relate to another person's needs and provide support if needed (and wanted). At the same time, the implications of our support regarding our own needs are being taken into consideration. This means that while you are solving a problem causing, for example, aggressive behaviour, your own goals are kept in mind and pursued, too, even when this is not obvious and mostly remains unnoticed by the person you are dealing with. This attitude allows you to explore the motives and needs of somebody else while staying aware of and putting them into perspective to your own goals. This also implies you automatically will change your attitude (or should) whenever an individual starts acting uncooperative or even gets too offensive and, therefore, contradicts the goal you are pursuing, like resolving the conflict. This attitude adapting to changing circumstances while dealing with aggressive people enables you to re-establish an adequate basis for a constructive dialogue. The nature of this rational attitude makes it also possible to quickly adjust your behaviour and take a more directing stance if needed. Also, by just reducing the leading component of your attitude and becoming more supportive, a communicative space on eye level is entered, where you can negotiate openly. It is more likely to find solutions on a participative level when the interaction is based on equal terms.

A distinct communicative attribute of this leading and supportive attitude is open questions like: "Can you tell me what it is about?"; "Can you tell me what the issue is?"; "I do not understand what it is about. Can you tell me?" It is not always required to concretely verbalise these questions. Typical nonverbal cues representing this benevolent mindset also indicate you are interested and want to provide support. With a leading and supportive attitude, you stay in control because the directing aspect of this attitude is not apparent, and you are not dominating the other person. The dynamics are being directed in a very subtle manner.

By asking straightforward what the issue is, it is suggested **there is an actual issue**. With this kind of questioning, a mental connection is established to a specific "unknown" need causing conflict and aggression and unconsciously motivating this individual to behave this way. This question automatically puts you into the position of the "helper", too, who leads the way to solve the problem and maybe already has a hypothetical solution in mind as well. Your counterpart takes on the role of the one in need of "help" and support. Most people stabilise themselves rather quickly, as soon as they are subjected to empathetic, leading, supportive effort and react constructively and cooperate. They presumably want the problem to be solved anyway but get lost in emotions and stress. Only seldomly do adverse reactions appear when you present yourself as being supportive and rational and staying in control over the situation when another person has 'lost it'. But in the end, the style of communication has to fit the person you are dealing with and the contextual circumstances you are in. It all comes down to your personal assessment of the situation. At all times, you must be able to adapt according to the development of the dynamics flexibly. Occasionally you will have to position yourself more with a defensive stance. Sometimes you need to go with the flow and take your time to "read" somebody. Or it can be necessary to shout or make a loud sound to distract someone or even demand somebody to stop what they are doing.

On a nonverbal physical level, the leading, supportive stance is noticeable by a self-secure, confident, upright, open posture while facing the other person directly. A slight step in the counterpart's direction and using asking and pointing gestures with arms and hands can also be beneficial.

Defensive attitude

By taking in a defensive position, you withdraw and disconnect from people and situations by turning inwardly. At the same time, external influences are being perceived critically. With this attitude, you can remain passive and show presence (first level intervention). If necessary, you can also deliver active (physical or mental) resistance to ward off negative external influences and impacts. The effects of this positioning make it possible to guard yourself mentally, physically and to re-claim personal needs if needed. A defensive stance is usually used as an assertive reaction towards pressure and the crossing of personal physical boundaries. You can draw and restore these boundaries by taking a self-confident step back and creating, marking and even claiming personal space by minimal an arm's length distance (second level intervention). In general, a defensive mindset is very effective against (subjective) intrusions and perceived* and realistic dangers.

The withdrawing oppositional, "rebellious", resistive and assertive behavioural characteristics of this mental attitude can be compared with being a soldier, digging a trench and actively delivering resistance and opposition (not passively sitting and waiting) against an attacking enemy. By taking on this position, you become more focused, centred on yourself and aware of your needs, and determined to define limits how far people can go. You demonstrate self-confidence and self-awareness considering your personal boundaries and therefore transmit concentrated power and sturdiness. The quality of communication is self-oriented, rigid and factual.

The following distinctive, nonverbal signs are typical for a defensive mindset: the arms are mainly folded if seated, the legs are mostly crossed, sparse physical movements or a static, rigid posture or defensive, physical gestures against physical attacks are demonstrated. Some direct their hand palms outwardly and symbolise and mark their boundaries.

*Our positioning depends on how we perceive social relations and interactions. This perception, however, can and often will be very subjective and biased by nature, and even phantasies and presumptions of what is expected could influence our positioning distinctively. This positioning based on, for example, presumptions is likely to affect how people again will react towards us. We then create something that is commonly also known as a "self-fulfilling prophecy". With a defensive attitude, it is important to realise this fact. You basically send out the message that you are being attacked. And how do you guess how "normal" but volatile and agitated people are going to react to this transferred expectation?

On a verbal level, defensive people use brief terse words, which are definite, assertive, defensive, disconnected, self-centred, and articulate with a low bass-like-voice inflexible and resistive messages, and call for respect regarding their needs and wants.

Cooperative attitude

This quality of attitude consists of both following and cooperative attributes. It implicates the enablement of the satisfaction of needs of the counterpart and therefore has implicit empathetic and social qualities. This can be advantageous but could also provide disadvantages notoriously when dealing with aggression. Taking on this position allows you to go along with the opposite person's efforts to satisfy their needs. This cooperative mindset is often used to maintain or build a social framework with other people. It is also an attitude used to prevent conflict when dealing with demanding people, for example. In this case, people go along and adjust to the insecure circumstances in a chameleon-like fashion. A dominant individual then controls and leads the interaction where they want to achieve their goals.

It can be disadvantageous to let people dominate and lead the interaction wherever they want to go. However, as long as people are aware of this fact and keep their own goal in mind, offensive people can also be led by creating space without them even noticing it. This is called leading by using a pulling (attraction) instead of using pushing (directing) force. It is also a significant advantage of this going along strategy to be able to avoid difficult and potentially unsolvable confrontations. Whenever it is not required to deal with a certain challenging individual for a prolonged period, like on the "street", it might not be worth it to put a lot of energy to try to adjust their attitude. In these cases, it really makes more sense to just go with the flow (with regard to your personal boundaries) to save energy and avoid a tedious confrontation. In social institutions or medical care facilities, this is much harder and not advisable. Problems with difficult people tend to accumulate in the long term, and at some point, they need to be professionally attended to.

Nonverbally this attitude distinguishes itself symbolically, but also concretely by a backwards-leaning posture; the body leans away and out of its axial centre with one leg mostly positioned backwards. The upper part of the body is flexed, with the positioning of the arms underlining this mental orientation to create distance from the occurrences. It signals the opening of personal space but also caution and readiness to withdraw (flee) physically in case an attack occurs. By this mindset related stance, a kind of vacuum (openness) is transferred. The space where the body is typically centred is now being left open, and the so-called intimate and personal zones are not represented and claimed and are left unguarded. In this empty unguarded space, an (aggressive) opposite individual is unconsciously drawn into it and will gain directing (dominating) force as a result. People opportunistically take on this complementary position because it is perceived as beneficial regarding their personal needs. But, as mentioned prior, if you tend to be a cooperative kind of person, it is possible to lead people by creating space and using pulling force if you stay aware of the goal you are aiming for. This isn't always easy when dealing with the personal boundary-crossing behaviour of certain individuals.

Offensive attitude

This quality of attitude consists of both attacking and competing characteristics. These are transmitted and communicated by distinct verbal and nonverbal messages we all are familiar with. When people position themselves offensively, the satisfaction of their personal needs is the most important and their main goal. The consequence of this attitude is that the needs of another person are not being considered. This causes pressure, and it often leads to feelings of frustration by those who feel negatively affected. Encounters with offensive people cause conflict in social relations and can even trigger an aggressive reaction in return.

The considerable advantage of an offensive mindset when de-escalating on some occasions is that it makes it possible to have an effective forceful influence upon turbulent, potentially dangerous evolving dynamics. Expressing a verbal offensive message can have an enormous disrupting and distracting influence on people and is likely to have a constructive impact – especially if confronted with expanding boundary-crossing aggression (third level intervention). An authentic offensive gesture could alter a situation drastically in your favour. After changing the "ball game" with a pinpoint offensive verbal action ("Stop this!"), control is taken over again, and the dynamics can be led in a constructive direction. High-stress levels resulting from the challenges then decline as soon as the control over the situation has been regained and the people change their behaviour for the better. This also allows you to shift position and show a different demeanour, if needed and when applicable, like leading and supporting. This combination of disrupting, distracting, and drawing attention with a verbal offensive gesture and then shifting into a secondary, more empathetic attitude, often positively affected the most difficult dynamics.

An offensive attitude should most certainly not be ruled out as a powerful tool to intervene in situations in which "milder" interventions have no effect. People sometimes are opposed to it because they only consider or are only acquainted with the negative sides commonly associated with "aggression". However, it should be acknowledged that an appropriately applied offensive gesture makes it possible to remain generally capable of acting in certain situations where people would feel helpless and powerless (experiencing power by making others feel helpless and powerless is a common theme regarding aggression). It also makes it possible to act assertively considering your personal needs, which generally are derived from the (professional) context in which you'll find yourself. An indirect effect of not losing the ability to act and thus not feeling helpless is that it enables one to remain empathetic towards the most challenging people. This can be important when you are structurally dealing with aggressive people like in certain professions (police, security services, mental institutions, hospitals etc.).

An offensive mentality is also required to deal with violent attacks of many kinds effectively. To ward off, for example, chokeholds and the aggressive grabbing of clothes, the focused power of this mindset is transferred and enables the necessary physical counteraction.

An offensive stance makes itself noticeable by distinct gesticulating signals ("finger-pointing"), but also due to the declining of physical distance and the crossing of personal boundaries. Offensive verbal messages are loud, direct, unempathetic and enforcing by nature. If an offensive action is misapplied and used disproportionally, these messages are what we normally call aggressive.

Step 3: Adjusting aggressive behaviour

The prior described qualities of attitudes can be used to de-escalate, restore crossed boundaries, prevent an escalation, and resolve conflict. Generally, interactions between people aren't static but instead very dynamic by nature. Reliable predictions of general outcomes, how people react, and what will happen next cannot realistically be made. What it really takes to deal with aggression in all its facets adequately and to resolve conflict is personal flexibility to adapt to the sometimes-rapid changes in circumstances and mental strategies to channel stress and control emotional impulses.

Offensive demanding behaviour

The best results in adjusting and balancing this form of aggression are achieved by taking in a passive defensive position and/or demonstrating presence (first level intervention). The intensity of this form of aggression is relatively low, and the invasiveness compared to other aggressions is marginal. Therefore, you can remain passive in your opposition. When you show presence or take on a more active defensive position (second level intervention) to balance this form of aggression, your boundaries will be transmitted and communicated clearly and confidently. It also allows you to resist the pressure better and raise awareness considering your personal needs by defining them verbally. By doing so, you probably will succeed to remain composed, and it also prevents possible impulsive reactions made out of frustration on your behalf. Offensive demanding behaviour puts you under pressure. Eventually, the effects will make you feel more agitated because this form of aggression has a "cornering" effect. Taking on a passive defensive position and/or actively setting boundaries is very effective against offensive demanding behaviour. Many actual experiences of my colleagues and myself have proved this. Most situations get balanced out rapidly, the tension drops on both sides, and the general dynamics eases.

However, it is also possible that the aggression increases in intensity, and it is necessary then to adapt your attitude again to match these new circumstances. This is also the case whenever people calm down and respect your boundaries. Perhaps this person needs a more supportive gesture on your behalf or even your cooperation to solve his problems. It generally makes sense to offer support after this initial inadequate approach has been balanced out. It prevents people from feeling left behind and feeling "disoriented", like in a kind of void or vacuum where they do not have a clue what to do next.

Aggression out of frustration can quickly happen if you do not provide any compensation by offering a perspective into his needs to be satisfied. For some people (children and juveniles, for example), it is hard to orientate themselves after their inadequate behaviour was abruptly stopped. They often do not find a compensating alternative by themselves to shift their attention onto some other goal and perspective. They tend to get progressively anxious, and this can trigger even more aggression.

If your stress level rises and your emotional impulses threaten to influence your actions, it is always a good option to go along with the dynamics. This will allow you to temporarily cope with the situation and prevent counterproductive impulsive reactions. By going along with the flow, you can gain some time and keep an overview of the situation. If you need even more information about the subject or it is necessary to plan a new strategy, you can also consciously continue to go along and observe. It creates time to process the information better. For the longer term, this adaptive, flexible, cooperative attitude is not always favourable and has, as pointed out before, some real disadvantages. Demanding people, especially children and juveniles, usually tend to unconsciously abuse situations without well-defined boundaries.

Aggressive manipulation

My experiences in dealing with both provocations and intimidations have shown promising results as soon as I reacted with a pronounced defensive stance (second level intervention) and then switched into a leading/supportive role. Defensive positioning makes it easier to resist aggressive manipulations and to deal with mental pressure. It helps to stay composed, guard your physical and psychological boundaries, and act assertively if needed. Of course, this sounds easier than it is going to be in reality. Each person has their own limits in successfully being able to resist aggressive manipulations. These limitations depend on a daily mood, (pre-existing) stress level and personal vulnerabilities. You will often find that these personal (temporary) dispositions and aspects of the self are opportunistically being put under direct pressure by these manipulating forces. Some people are absolute masters in sensing these personal vulnerabilities. If you feel overwhelmed and emotional impulses threaten to influence your actions, it is an option to withdraw completely or look for help.

A defensive mindset and resistive positioning have their advantages when dealing with this kind of challenging manipulative people over a more extended period, like at a workplace or when dealing with clients in a social institution. In other cases, it might be better or easier to avoid these people.

As soon as you claim and defend your boundaries in a self-confident manner by using the typical assertive verbal and nonverbal messages (stop-signal), you will notice a change of behaviour. In most cases, the aggressor calms down, and his behaviour changes for the better, which means your boundaries are respected. Manipulative people are more or less still in control over themselves and their actions. Some just leave the scene in an agitated manner whilst swearing and shouting. For me, this isn't a problem as long as they do not hurt themselves or others.

As soon as people have calmed down, you can choose to shift into the leading and supporting role. By doing so, control over the situation is regained. You can lead this person subtly without putting them under too much pressure. You will likely be able to provide support to some extent. In the meantime, this outcome will probably also fit your personal or professional goals. The next step of using verbal de-escalating techniques in the following chapter presents the necessary special skills to make people aware of the actual motivations causing their aggressive behaviour.

A manipulative person can sometimes react with frustration in case boundaries are being set. This is noticed quite quickly, as aggression out of frustration is an entirely different form of "aggression" with distinct features. Instead of intentionally trying to manipulate you, a frustrated person acts out overtly in a very agitated, impulsive, highly emotional uncontrolled manner without paying too much attention to you. In some cases, a highly frustrated person could completely lose self-control. Always avoid putting a highly frustrated person under additional pressure or instigating any negative influences. It could trigger impulsive, defensive or even intentional violence.

It is generally required to constantly adapt your actions and attitude to the form of aggression you are confronted with. When you have gained more experience dealing with specific individuals, you will notice some obvious patterns regarding their (aggressive) behaviour and conflict themes. It makes it somewhat predictable what to expect, and it makes it, to some extent, easier to deal with the challenges since you are slightly more prepared. But still, you should remain cautious and beware of becoming too complacent.

As a basic rule, it is safer to remind yourself that aggression can change rapidly as time proceeds and circumstances change. The outcome of these kinds of dynamics is and will always be somewhat unpredictable and should be treated with respect. To "expect the unexpected" is an important general mindset, but it is also very demanding for most people, especially regarding aggression. It calls for a lot of experience and mental strength to deal with this kind of uncertainty and still be able to keep an open mind in real, potentially life-threatening situations. Nevertheless, it is something that can be learned by training to use your physical (self-defence) and mental capabilities ("reading" of people and situations, generating mental strength) effectively. By gaining such self-knowledge and skills, while at the same time considering tendencies to certain kinds of reactions and personal limitations, allows you to stay more focused. Even if you reach your limit, it is always possible to remain on the safe side by following and returning to the basic rules in dealing with dangerous encounters, like getting help and looking for a safe exit.

Aggressive acts out of frustration

This aggression mainly concerns the aggressor who (repeatedly) gets frustrated or is highly stressed, to begin with, even though we will feel under massive pressure by this behaviour. This form of aggression is likely to cause anxiety, fear, feelings of helplessness, and sometimes anger. With people acting out aggressively, it is probable to have caused these strong reactions yourself because you dealt with a situation in a certain way and triggered a conflict. Frustrated behaviour due to a conflict, however, cannot always be prevented. Structurally avoiding conflicts is an unrealistic (and unhealthy) ambition. Frustrations are likely to happen and are considered a normal part of life. We all must eventually learn to deal with unsatisfying situations to build a healthy resilience to these kinds of life events. Even then, we sometimes still will react too strongly and aggressively when our expectations are not met. This said, acting out in frustration is always a person's way of dealing with their own (they own them) frustrations and is related to somebody's personality traits and state.

In many situations, the possibilities to actively influence a highly frustrated individual are limited. It is advisable to take on a reserved position and mentally guard yourself and not absorb the negative energy. Sometimes you can find yourself being (mis-)used as a kind of "lightning rod". Highly frustrated people tend to project their negative images and anger onto opposites. It is intricate and often impossible to be much of a constructive help when somebody is highly agitated and emotionally unstable. Maybe this situation could have been prevented by being more aware of the implications of denying a need or refusing to cooperate. Decisions, however, are generally made because they are of importance regarding professional tasks or personal needs. These demands can and will occasionally contradict somebody else's ideas of how things should be. This leads to conflicts and possible adverse reactions.

When somebody loses their temper and starts acting out by being verbally abusive, hostile and by shouting, etc., it is important to first take on a passive, defensive position (first level intervention) and create enough distance between you and this person. If you are less of a target (this person is not shouting directly at you and his attention and focus are somewhere else), a more open observing position could help regain a better overview. It makes it possible to estimate the danger level or plan or rethink a strategy (like getting help, alarming people etc.). Generally, a passive defensive attitude and being with oneself helps to "outlive", overcome and withstand these problematic predicaments. In some cases, it is also a good option to withdraw to maintain basic personal security.

As time passes by, the level of excitement is going to decline due to natural exhaustion. As soon as this person progressively calms himself down, the emotions stabilise as well. At some point, he will be able to reason again. As long as there is no real danger to you or to somebody else like close colleagues or innocent bystanders, you can outlast the situation by making use of time. If people suddenly start massively destroying material objects, this should make you warier of the fact that this individual might oppose a real danger and become violent. Such developments, of course, make it more challenging to stay calm and composed. These dangerous situations will automatically affect you more profoundly. It is then even more important to regulate stress and stay focused. Always trust your instincts and take these internal warning signals seriously to stay safe.

In specific jobs, like in social or mental institutions and hospitals, it can be necessary to discuss alternatives to adopt better strategies to deal with feelings of frustration. Also, it can be helpful to discuss how this situation occurred in the first place and what made this individual behave as they did. However, this discussion of past experiences and future strategies should be done as soon as the aggressor has sufficiently calmed down to prevent any new build-up of tension and causing irritations.

A typical aspect of social relations needs to be considered responsible for making highly frustrated individuals become dangerous. Especially people under the influence of stress feel like they always have to actively influence situations and support others to achieve results. This is often seen in fields of work where the supportive role is a part of the general professional attitude and working moral (socially related jobs). Some find it very hard not to respond to such occurrences. It can be a challenge to take in a more passive role, just to be with yourself and outlast the situation. Acting upon frustrated individuals could instigate real problems. "I cannot let somebody vent his tension like this and act out his emotions, can I?"; "I must do something to help!". These are some of the basic examples to underline what I exactly mean. These inappropriate actions often find an origin in the insecurity and the personal needs of these persons themselves ("I must do something, shouldn't I?"; "What will other people or my boss think of me, when I leave it like that and do not intervene?") These overreactions seldom have a constructive outcome when dealing with highly frustrated individuals who, like in most cases, cannot accept support, even when it comes with the best intentions. On the contrary, these personally motivated and well-meant reactions could easily be experienced as additional demands and put an aggressive person under more pressure. As a result, the tension is going to increase furthermore and probably trigger an hostile reaction. It will be even more dangerous when supportive people start making physical contact and "try" to calm somebody down that way. You will find generally that most frustrated individuals, especially adults, really want to be left alone. But at the same time (this is contradictory and makes it sometimes very complicated), they also "need" people to be around in the function of negative objects to project their anger onto.

Suppose a frustrated person is acting out but doesn't actually transmit any need for support. In that case, it is safer and more effective to endure the turbulent situation because:

1. It helps in not providing a stage for the aggressor.
2. It brings the possible feeding with extra attention to a halt from which additional energy could be drawn, making aggressive behaviour generally last longer.
3. It is often useful to represent a (passive) calm, grounded, substantial entity offering this "derailed" individual some orientation.

By following these principles, you will exercise an indirect constructive influence. It simply is not always required to be obviously active to achieve certain goals. The symbolic content of what you represent with your presence ("I am here and have it under control", "No worries, you will be fine") can have an even more enormous impact compared to verbal interventions.

Intentional physical violence

Because of the nature of this form of aggression, the rapid mode of action and the high danger level, there will be little time and space to adjust this kind of violence and act constructively. The most important thing is always to guard your physical safety. Suppose the imminent danger of physical violence has been recognised, and you still can decide what to do. In that case, it is of the utmost importance to control stress, leave the situation, and get help (colleagues, police, and security personal). In case you find yourself being cornered; the basic rule is to avoid a physical confrontation until you see an opportunity to get yourself to safety.

If somebody launches a direct physical attack, it is hard to predict how somebody will react. Instincts will trigger fight-fight-freeze reflexes. Because of this fact, it makes no real sense for me to advise what type of response is most suitable to deal with this extreme form of aggression. What I can say out of my own experience, however, is that reactions to physical violence can be influenced by the degree of training one has in dealing with attacks like chokeholds and punches. It is also important to mobilise at least a defensive but also an offensive mentality. The difference between both is that with defensive reactions, you offer resistance and then withdraw. With offensive actions, you go forward, (counter-) attack and (try to) take over (control).

Learning practical skills and martial arts to deal with attacks is one thing. Using these techniques on other humans and possibly causing nasty injuries is another. To be effective in applying self-defensive abilities, it is necessary to disconnect from one's empathetic feelings and from everyday social and moral standards of how we usually interact with other people. Then you can act with physical defensive or offensive tactics and do what you need to do to remain secure.

During my training, I experienced that "aggression" is hardly ever perceived as beneficial. Sometimes, however, aggression is necessary and positive. A lot of people haven't connected to their personal aggressive potential because these traits are integral to their perceived self. Mostly you'll find that these aspects are being suppressed. It is a common mechanism to deal with personality traits that could make you feel insecure. This principle could also potentially cause even more problems, as these aspects are still there, lingering around, waiting to emerge under the "right" circumstances, most likely in an uncontrolled, disproportional fashion causing harmful effects.

The fact is that our aggression or integrated defensive and offensive qualities of mental attitude can provide us with basic physical security and have other constructive effects in human interactions, like being able to set boundaries. To apply defensive and offensive capabilities constructively, it is required to get to know them and learn how to use them in which conditions. And even then, every individual will have their own tendencies in reacting overly aggressive depending on personal characteristics and the context in which interactions with other people take place.

The next step

The next step in dealing with aggression is to de-escalate verbally and to try to resolve conflict. In this stage, the starting point is that you establish a decent usable connection to this individual. It is necessary to be on "eye level" to find solutions with the help of verbal de-escalating skills effectively. This stage is critical, as someone can swiftly turn aggressive again. It would be best if you acted in a self-confident way while remaining cautious at the same time.

Summary

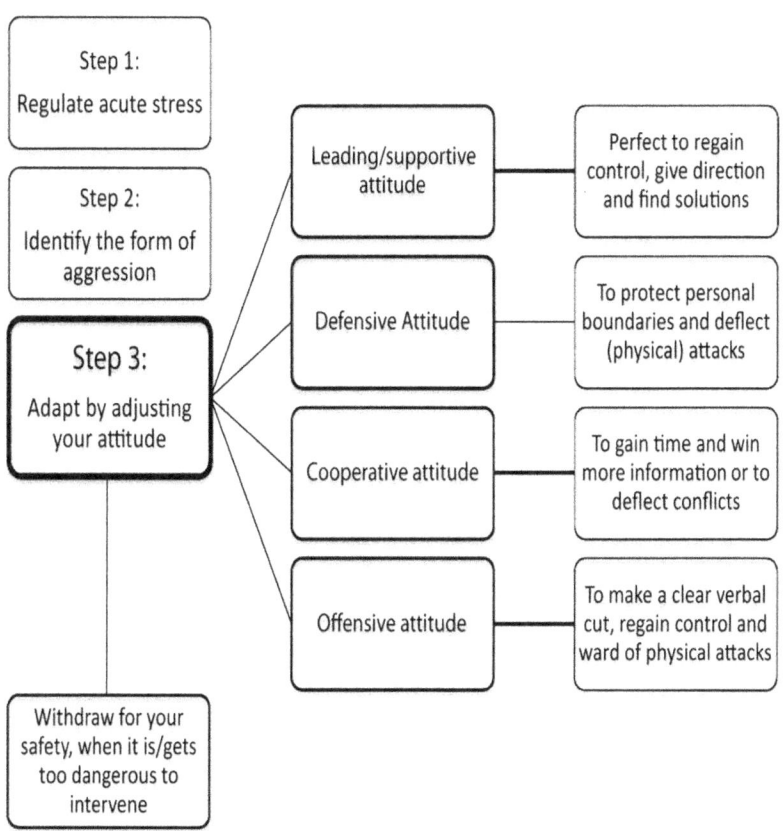

Step 1:
Regulate acute stress

Step 2:
Identify the form of aggression

Step 3:
Adapt by adjusting your attitude

Leading/supportive attitude

Perfect to regain control, give direction and find solutions

Defensive Attitude

To protect personal boundaries and deflect (physical) attacks

Cooperative attitude

To gain time and win more information or to deflect conflicts

Offensive attitude

To make a clear verbal cut, regain control and ward of physical attacks

Withdraw for your safety, when it is/gets too dangerous to intervene

Exercise five: getting to know qualities of mental attitudes

The exercise is first to describe your estimations of your own general quality of predominant attitude under specific circumstances like at work or home. Then estimate the attitude you are confronted with in the same context. You could also be more specific and reflect interactions with individual people like, for example, at your work. After this, you can assess whether the qualities of attitude regarding yourself and those of others in the same situations are complementary or not. Complementary attitudes or mirroring types of attitudes create a balance in interactions because they possess opposite attributes. The most common examples for this are offensive and defensive attitudes or leading and following.

These estimations of personal attitudes in certain situations will be subjective by nature, and attitudes will not always prove to be complementary, but this is not the point. It is important to raise your awareness considering your personal attitude under various circumstances and to find out what kind of attitude you are confronted with, making, causing or even forcing you to take in a certain quality of attitude, which is, of course, always related to your personality traits. You could also do it the other way around and directly connect your attitude to a complementary quality of attitude as described below, and seriously reflect whether this conclusion is representative of the actual situation or not.

The basic four qualities of attitude:

- ➢ Rational (leading, supportive)
- ➢ "Going along" (following, cooperative)
- ➢ Offensive (attacking, competing)
- ➢ Defensive (delivering resistance, withdrawing)

The complementary qualities of attitudes are:

Rational (leading, supportive) and "Going along" (following, cooperative) attitude.

Offensive (attacking, competing) and Defensive (delivering resistance, withdrawing) attitude.

You could also consider these following opposing positions, as they probably need no further explanation:

Dominant (demanding) versus submissive (following) positioning.

It can be hard to distinguish between so-called "mirroring" or complementary qualities of attitude, but there are big differences. People tend to mix up qualities of attitude whenever they try to determine their tendencies. Some examples indicating how small and subtle the differences can be:

➤ "I can do this for you if you want me to" or "I am here if you need any help" is a going along/cooperative attitude because the initiative lies with your counterpart who can make use of your willingness to cooperate.

➤ "What do you need?" or "How can I help you?" on the other hand, is a supportive, leading attitude. Here you take the initiative and suggest there is a need for support to accomplish a defined task, and the execution of this is already determined and not an "if" anymore. The actual execution of the task is the main goal for the person showing this attitude. The difference is not that obvious but substantial.

➤ "I demand you do this!" or "Do this!" is clearly offensive.

➤ ""Stop doing this!" is a defensive reaction on (subjectively perceived) an intrusion or hostility.

The exercise:

General description of a situation:
My attitude in this specific situation:
The attitude I find myself confronted with:
Are these attitudes complementary?
☐ yes   ☐ no

*Additional exercise templates can be found on page 139

4. Basic principles of verbal de-escalating techniques

During the progressive development of aggressive dynamics, various phases can be distinguished. Each separate phase represents possibilities, as well as impossibilities, potential problems and even dangers considering the use of verbal de-escalating techniques. A precise determination of the actual phase is therefore necessary. These sometimes rapidly changing, succeeding phases are related to the level of agitation as it increases and will decrease over time. Occasionally, the first phases even are (apparently) bypassed. This causes real challenges, as you can be caught by surprise. It implies, for example, that in an instant, seemingly "harmless" and balanced people could become violent due to the slightest conflict.

Typical physical symptoms and behavioural cues accompany the escalating phases, which usually correspond with the level of stress and agitation. As the internal pressure increases, the behavioural cues and physical symptoms will change. In some perilous situations, however, there are hardly any signals and cues which could raise our awareness and attention. This could be the case with potentially violent people willing to use this force intentionally. Their tension level is high, but they are focused and concentrated and relatively calm, reserved, composed, and less restless. Then no real obvious signs for imminent danger can be observed. People contemplating using violence prepare themselves to execute a violent act mentally by planning or visualising pictures and will carry this out if and when they see fit to do so (you see this also with people planning to commit suicide).

Some people also effectively control themselves over a more extended period, even when their tension is internally very high. This can be the case with people who are used to being under the influence of stress. They show hardly any signs of imminent overt aggression. At some point, for example, due to a conflict, their control mechanisms could fail, resulting in impulsive, aggressive actions that come out of the blue.

To be effective with verbal de-escalating techniques and stay safe during the process, it is important to make yourself aware of the actual phase you are in with this person. This is also necessary because the conversational approach needs to be adjusted in each different phase.

Your counterpart should be capable of processing, understanding, and giving meaning to the verbal contents with their cognitive resources. This individual must be able to think and reflect about what you are saying and make decisions according to their own understanding.

The quality of cognitive functioning is inversely related to the level of stress. Therefore, the capabilities to think and perceive messages is related to the escalating phases of aggressive dynamics. An increase in stress will mean that the quality of cognitive functioning and the ability to process information properly is going to decline. With each next escalation phase, people are less likely to reflect and control their emotions and impulses. This points out the reason why the content of the expressed messages at least needs to be adapted to enable a stressed-out individual to understand what you are trying to say. For example, forming elementary, unambiguous short sentences is absolutely required in the escalating phase of aggressive dynamics. For a highly agitated person, this would make it principally possible to still process the expressed words. You also prevent demanding too much and causing additional stress and anger, which could easily escalate. Long ambiguous, complicated messages should never be used in this stage.

However, verbal de-escalating techniques cannot be effective anymore when the tension level has reached a certain point (this can be different from person to person). When in doubt, you should first try to make eye contact and see if this person is able to shift his attention. Being able to establish eye contact means the cognitive capabilities are sufficient for **basic** verbal communication. If not, refrain from further trying and wait until it is possible again while paying attention to the general safety of all people involved and maybe deciding to get help.

Escalating phases – sometimes it is better not to speak.

The model describing the escalating phases (page 86) originally is called "the 5 Phases of Escalation" (G. Breakwell, 1997). The starting point in this model is a zeroing reference line representing so-called "common behaviour" regarding an individual. This reference line is beneficial. It raises your awareness considering any behavioural changes. "Common behaviour" is not the same and should not be interpreted as so-called "normal social behaviour". The average way an individual behaves is defined as being "common" for this specific person. To assess an average value regarding behavioural tendencies, it is necessary to consider social, cultural, individual dispositions and properties, as well as unique temperament and the ways someone commonly expresses himself. Only then can you really distinguish between any significant change and distinctive developments to more destructive tendencies. Some people are just more energised and impulsive by nature and show an above-average temperament.

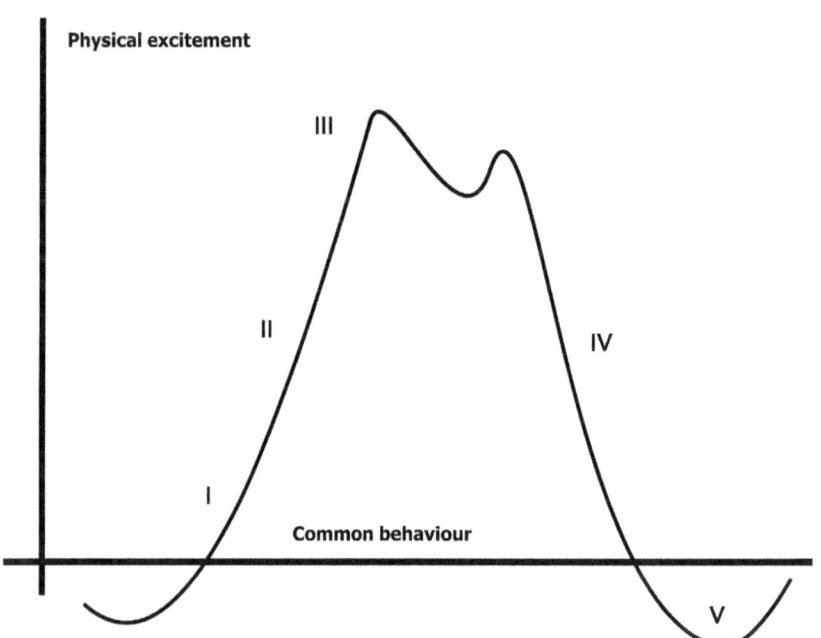

4.1 The 5 Phases of Escalation, Breakwell 1997

Others are less proficient in communicating, and some people verbally express and pronounce themselves structurally ungracious and harsh. These characteristics belong to these individuals and have to be seen as attributes regarding their "common behaviour".

In most cases, it is not difficult to discern this so-called "common way" in which an individual behaves. You can get a good impression of how people normally are and observe a distinct change in behaviour. Nevertheless, sometimes an escalation is not going to build up in stages or phases. Occasionally, individuals who are always tensed-up due to chronic work-related stress or trauma, for example, are well experienced in controlling their physical and emotional pressure over an extended period of time. Therefore, outsiders perceive them as balanced because they continuously are in this state. In these cases, no or only a few subtle signs can be observed that indicate that this person is under enormous emotional pressure and struggle to control themselves (i.e., avoiding certain situations and conflict). However, the reactions and the way people act in social relations are sometimes good indicators of how people truly feel and what state they are in. In these cases, only a minor conflict or additional pressure could easily trigger a massive hostile reaction. These situations are potentially perilous as highly tensed-up people are likely to lose their self-control. It also overwhelms those involved, catching them by surprise and having difficulty linking the conflict itself and the disproportionate aggressive reaction.

The phases of aggressive dynamics

The **first phase** in aggression dynamics in social relations is called the **triggering or initiating phase**. In this phase, the attitude changes significantly compared to common behaviour (with most people, some are seemingly permanently in the initiating phase). In the triggering phase, people can still be well reached with verbal de-escalating interventions, as they are very well in control over their impulses. The tension level is already increased in comparison to being in a balanced state. Subtle physical symptoms like an increased muscle tone and breathing frequency, general, motoric restlessness and sweating are typical for this phase. On a communicative level, people show a more hostile demeanour. Crossing personal boundaries by verbal messages and physical actions is possible, as well as expressing demands (also sub-textual) and explicit threats and insults to intimidate or provoke. The voice gets louder and the tone higher. These are all signs indicating this person is in a more offensive state of mind.

In this phase, the further development of the dynamics largely depends on whether the proper interventions are applied, and control is regained. Not intervening could cause a further escalation, but some also calm down on their own. In this phase of the build-up of aggressive dynamics, people could also show signs of withdrawal or avoid having social interactions altogether. However, withdrawal is also a tell-tale and distinctive sign of a behaviour change, indicating a build-up of tension, anxiety and potential aggression. Bodily features that are representative of a heightened physical agitation are notoriously hard to hide or control. They probably remain observable and could serve as valuable signs and important cues, even if somebody internally manages to control himself. It is important to take this behaviour change seriously by, for example, making contact with this person. If these (sparse) cues remain unnoticed or are overseen, negative emotions could pent-up and internally, this person already is in the next phase, albeit not showing it overtly. This will mean you will probably be confronted with very aggressive offensive actions triggered by a minor conflict, which usually leads to massive challenges.

Dealing with this kind of overt aggression in the next phase is more complicated and dangerous than in a situation where the tension level is less high, like in the initiating phase. Also, the probability of direct violent acts is less likely in an early stage of the dynamics. In this first phase, aggressive forms like demanding behaviour and offensive manipulations often occur. Also, if an already tense and unstable person experiences other conflict or frustration in this stage, impulsive aggressive reactions are a realistic possibility. The tell-tale signs representing the first phase of aggressive dynamics can be very subtle and hard to distinguish, especially when in chaotic and demanding situations with a lot going on. These obvious signals will primarily draw your attention. However, your gut feelings or intuition can still help you pick up subtle cues in the background.

The **second phase** is called the **escalating phase**. In this stage, the cognitive capabilities are significantly reduced. Verbal de-escalating intervention is possible, but the content and communication style must be adopted to succeed. Only short unambiguous sentences should be formulated and used. It is also important to make no additional demands on your behalf. This would cause a further increase in tension. On the other hand, crossed personal boundaries need to be restored before you start the conversation. For building a constructive dialogue, it is important to be on eye level.

The physical and behavioural characteristics of the escalating phase are more pronounced and distinct. For example, threats and insults are invasive, highly provocative and intimidating. Physical boundaries of involved people or bystanders are no longer being respected, and the damaging of property is to be expected. A transition into the next phase and, therefore, a total loss of self-control can happen. It is crucial to be aware of possible physical attacks and, for your personal safety, to respect the realistic danger of this situation. Basis rules for dealing with unstable and highly agitated people must always be followed, like having a secure way out.

In this second phase, it is further possible that stress and negative emotions are still being effectively controlled internally by the aggressor. A sudden transition into the next destructive phase at the slightest instance is very much possible. Situations like these are dangerous as it is unlikely that people can control their aggressive impulses. In these situations, violent actions are a risk. If caught by surprise, a flight-or-fight response and impulsive actions are more likely to occur too.

The **third phase** is called the **crisis phase.** In this stage, the cognitive capabilities to process information are reduced to a minimum, and the behaviour is highly impulsive and aggressive. Interventions with verbal de-escalating techniques cannot be effective anymore. Trying to involve people in having a dialogue in this phase could easily lead to an escalation. People are likely to project their hate and anger directly onto you and lose self-control if confronted with irritating demands, like verbal interventions. The risk of physical attacks is genuine and realistic due to the high level of tension and the distinct reduced capabilities to control aggressive impulses.

Keeping yourself and others safe (people unaware of the situation or cannot defend themselves, like children) is now the most crucial task. Options to deal with this situation are minimal and depend on the (professional) context and circumstances. Basic examples for safety strategies are: keeping a safe distance or creating distance, arranging support or, like in some professions, using physical restraining and controlling techniques. If you get attacked, it is vital to defend yourself to prevent you from being physically injured or worse. Being able to defend yourself also helps to prevent suffering from excessive psychological negative consequences caused by feeling helpless and powerless.

A typical characteristic of the **fourth phase**, the **recovery phase,** is the reduced tension level. An aggressive, emotional outburst eventually leads to physical exhaustion. The capability to think, the content of what is being expressed and the mode of verbal communication will normalise in this phase. In the recovery phase, typical physical signs and other signals indicate the internal pressure has reduced:

> ➢ the muscle tone normalises with the declining of the adrenalin level in the blood
> ➢ the facial colour returns to normal
> ➢ the motoric restlessness and physical excitement decrease

> communicating reasonably is also possible again

It is crucial to be aware of the real risk of a sudden and rapid increase of agitation caused by internal and external influences. In the blink of an eye, you can find yourself in the middle of a crisis again. I have seen this often. These avoidable counterproductive influences are, for example, negative stimulations caused by verbally addressing delicate themes and provocations by other people. A supportive, cautious approach and a room with few stimuli are preferred and generally beneficial.

The **fifth and last** is the **depression phase,** in which aggressive people are wholly depleted from energy and exhausted. This leaves them in an empty, depressed state of being. Some feel ashamed and remorse because of their actions, but others still have hateful, hostile thoughts as they think injustice was done to them. The content of the communication style will generally normalise. This is the right moment for a debriefing of the past occurrences with all people involved. An evaluation with the aggressive individual (if applicable, like in social institutions and hospitals) takes place sometime later because they are usually not ready to talk directly after a crisis. The main goal is to prevent future conflicts and aggression. In some professions, debriefings are sometimes difficult to organise and regularly are just forgotten. On many occasions, I experienced those involved not always available to help de-escalate the situation, and some even left for home. An assigned person should be considered to prevent this important part from being left out of the occasion.

Basic rules for conducting verbal de-escalating techniques

The main goal of a verbal intervention is always to try to influence the dynamics rather than the individual personally. Also, the person you are having this conversation with at least must get the impression you are willing to **help satisfy his needs**. By showing this attitude, his willingness to cooperate increases and the risk of an adverse reaction decreases. A supportive, leading, empathetic attitude is ideal for achieving this effect. In comparison, enforcing personal needs and exerting additional pressure while disregarding your counterpart's needs would most probably lead to frustration.

Keeping a leading role and staying focused on your goal of solving conflict is a real advantage, even if it is applied very subtly. The aggressor will unconsciously follow their less constructive goal as they are still in a "battle" mode. When we keep this in mind, it is apparent why it is so important to keep a leading role and, when lost, to regain it. On the other hand, and this is mostly the more difficult part, it is also necessary to stay aware of or at least not to disregard the needs of this other individual.

At the beginning of the conversation, it is important to establish a **relationship with the opposite person based on trust**. It is not a good idea to be too hasty in attempting to lead the conversation. This could pose a real problem. Taking on a leading position and directing the conversation initially without having a decent relationship could also easily cause a power struggle or a conflict. Especially, unknown people in a conflict mode do not like to be directed, dominated or told "what to do" by some stranger. A balanced relationship based on equality is significant in the early stages of verbal de-escalating intervention. A power struggle in this phase is not going to be of any help.

The basic rules for conducting a constructive conversation are:

> ➢ approach and connect
> ➢ build a relationship on one's eye level. Adjust aggressive behaviour, if necessary.
> ➢ lead the conversation and offer support.
> ➢ always stay aware of the goal you are pursuing.

In the previous section, I mentioned the importance of having **goals**. Before starting with the actual conversation or even generally at work, in case you can expect conflict and aggression, you should have a clear picture in mind of what you want to achieve. These mental pictures are of importance to prevent you from acting like a ship in a storm without a captain. Whenever you are aware of the goal you are going to pursue, this implies you have set a (mental) compass and know which direction you want to go with the conversation. You then will act accordingly.

Generally, but especially when trying to establish a constructive dialogue and for de-escalating a situation and staying safe, it is important to **define both an optimum and a minimum goal**. An optimum goal represents your main course of direction, like achieving a conversation on eye level. Staying safe should always be a minimum goal in these kinds of situations. This minimum goal becomes relevant as soon as people you are dealing with are, for example, non-compliant and start behaving aggressively. This behaviour then activates a different, more security-related mindset.

As soon as you achieve your goal of de-escalating the situation, you lead the conversation according to a minimum and optimum work-related goal. Usually, these objectives originate from contextual (professional) circumstances and should be solution-oriented. An example of a general work-related optimum goal could be completely solving the problem or envisioning someone being cooperative. Minimum goals could be to offer emotional support in case you cannot solve the real problem. Also, someone no longer disturbing your class could be a minimum goal you can envision achieving.

If you only had one main goal in mind in this stage of the conversation that **has to be** achieved at all costs, this will lead to fixation and a loss of flexibility. Your counterpart is probably incapable of exactly fulfilling the expectations you envisioned. This most certainly causes conflict, a power struggle and even an escalation. It also poses a real risk to start exerting additional pressure on an already tense and emotionally unstable counterpart into achieving this goal you are fixated on. It also makes it more complicated, if not impossible, to de-escalate this situation. So, maintaining certain flexibility is always a good thing, like being on eye level with your counterpart and trying to find a solution that will suit both parties. Rigid and inflexible positioning makes it almost impossible to establish any decent base for regular dialogue. Any hard work you put into creating a balance in the relationship will be lost, and together with it, so will the trust and goodwill of your counterpart. You most likely will have to start all over again.

Precedents are commonly used to enforce the satisfaction of a specific personal need. The confrontation with an individual mentioning past occurrences and the opportunities given by other people to satisfy his needs (for example, with colleagues) creates an impression and feeling that if you would decide not to grant their wants, you are maltreating this person. Most people want to prevent becoming exposed to a situation in which they are being confronted with the fact they maltreated somebody by making some decision. This is regarded as being "on trial". What makes it also challenging to decide how to react to a precedent is the emerging of a kind of internal conflict; you do not want to give up your needs by deciding in favour of another demanding person because this implies and causes feelings of frustration.

Mentioning precedents is a subtle (probably not conscious) form of manipulation directed at your conscience and personal understanding of morals. Precedents could make you feel very insecure about how to deal with this occasion. This insecurity could prove to be in favour of this individual mentioning a precedent to achieve goals. As with all forms of manipulations, pointing out precedents and the accompanying enforcing arguments are about controlling people and situations and exerting certain power.

By quoting a precedent, somebody insists you must give in to meet his demands. This perceived subjective right to demand that you have to comply is based on (allegedly) past (similar) situations. The starting point motivating somebody to express precedents is insecurity that his demands will be declined, or at least he has concerns about how you are going to react.

When dealing with precedents, you should remember that although situations can be alike, each new event is always one of a kind and unique; the similarity is not a reason to ask for or even demand immediate cooperation. The facts speak for themselves; both occasions **are** different. This is a good argument you could use and a fundamental point you can refer to. This makes it possible to (re-)define boundaries in a self-conscious manner, and it gets you back in control (for now).

Deciding to cooperate based on a verbalised precedent probably leads to even more complicated situations in the future. Especially in social institutions, schools and medical facilities, this happens a lot. This reaction implicitly implies a confirmation and a corroboration of the subjective assumption of righteousness. It leads to and enforces future expectations. Cooperating on the premises of precedents has a learning and rewarding effect. If it is necessary to decline cooperation on a future occasion, this will be much harder and create massive conflict. Also, people likely start behaving aggressively into forcing you to cooperate and meet the expectations. This individual is going to be more frustrated in case his demands are ultimately denied.

In case you are being confronted with precedents, I can advise you to **clearly point out** that past situations do not constitute validity to claim cooperation on this occasion. By taking on this defensive stance, your own needs are not going to get compromised while the positions are being (re-) defined. You will probably get on eye level again. This is a good solid base for the next round of talks to find a solution. The dynamics could escalate by defining your boundaries too. However, this potential to act with even more aggression already exists in the first place. Triggering aggressive reactions and conflicts cannot always be avoided. In this new situation, you need to adapt and use other interventions depending on what you are being confronted with, like people acting out of frustration or trying to manipulate you. Going along could be a good solution to prevent an escalation. However, this strategy should only occasionally be used and is generally not advisable in case social relations prolong. People get accustomed to this very quickly, and this generates future expectations.

Making **promises** could lead to conflicts and can trigger aggression if you are not able to live up to them. This can occur as circumstances are not always under your control. I always act with reserve and rarely make any promises. In most cases, it is sufficient to assure that you will do everything in your power to help someone (as long as this also matches your goals). Providing somebody with the impression that their motives are being taken seriously benefits in having a postponing effect regarding having their needs satisfied.

Another important basic rule is to always **stick to the truth**. It may be tempting to lie from the best intentions, take a shortcut into reaching a certain goal and get out of this straining situation. However, the risk of being caught in a lie during the negotiation is too high, and the consequences will be severe. It will also get more difficult to have an open discussion with somebody when you constantly need to maintain the cover story. It is nearly impossible to prevent getting caught lying. The mechanisms eventually leading to the truth are uncontrollable.

A final golden rule is to always conduct a de-escalating negotiation with **only one person**. This is one of the main rules, which is nevertheless often ignored or forgotten under stressful circumstances. A second person is there to intervene in the event of a physical attack. They should refrain from taking on an active part, while you are in the midst of having a de-escalating conversation. Interfering in this stage would make the situation much more complicated and confusing. This negative consequence should always be avoided. You could easily push people over the edge.

A partner could take over the conversation whenever the first one is not able to establish a constructive dialogue, or he gets too stressed out. Sometimes people also project persisting negative images onto others. Then it will be hard to interact constructively and solve any problems. This is the right moment to take over the negotiations in a clear-cut manner.

The basic content of a de-escalating conversation

The typical characteristics of aggressive behaviour usually draw our attention. We tend to fixate on these unmistakable unfavourable and adverse signals. As a result, our responses are mainly determined by these occurrences, especially if we are no longer with ourselves due to stress and anxiety. However, to efficiently conduct a de-escalating conversation and be able to find solutions for underlying problems, it is required to focus on the motivation and the needs causing conflict and aggressive behaviour and not on the aggression itself. Before you can get to this stage, first, you regain your composure and try to get on eye level with your counterpart. Aggressive acts done out of frustration have to be endured until people become exhausted, as long as you are capable of handling them safely. The level of tension first has to decline to have a chance at building a constructive relationship. Also, the verbal contents cannot be processed adequately when people are highly agitated and emotional.

When people have calmed down, they often still express one-way demands. Based on these claims, it is very difficult to find solutions that are satisfying for both parties. A demand is a one-way urge to have personal needs met. Reacting to this behaviour by expressing demands yourself and therefore not cooperating as was anticipated tends to immediately cause a power struggle. Then both parties take on a defensive position and try to convince the other by applying pressure and stating undifferentiated, selfish arguments. On the other hand, a known motive provides us with many possibilities and options to find solutions. It gives us more room for negotiating. Focusing on these underlying motives usually leads to a solution-oriented conversation where both sides can be considered and respected.

Exploring needs and motivations to find solutions

During a de-escalating dialogue, it is not advantageous to try to explore the deeper causes of sometimes structurally dysfunctional and challenging behaviour. The main goal is and should be to find an acceptable solution in the "now". It is important to contemplate possible causes in the back of your mind whilst forming an opinion about the situation as a whole. However, these factors should not play a significant role during the actual conversation. Fixating on these elements and contemplating them too much could be distractive, making the process even more complicated.

These aspects causing conflict and aggression can be considered and even used to prevent future "derailments" after this primary task of finding a solution has been accomplished and the problem has been solved.

How to bring motives into mind.

To build a constructive dialogue based on the personal needs of an individual, the following aspects are important:

> Content analysis
> Pay attention to the nonverbal signs of expression
> Perceive the transferred information in its contextual entirety

Content analysis

For gathering useful information, it is necessary to strive for an objective perception of what has been said and what triggered the conflict and aggression in the first place. In other words, it is important to perceive what personal needs and motivations are "obscured" by agitated and aggressive behaviour. Building a clear, unbiased understanding of what the concerns are is of the utmost importance. Guesses, estimates and personal projections of what somebody's concerns possibly could be are to be prevented.

To be able to understand what somebody says and what his needs are, consider the following:

> listen, while letting your speaking partner speak out and give him the time to complete his sentences
> take your time to process the content
> use your intuition
> try to stay objective

Listening and associating simultaneously is counterproductive for being able to understand what this person is trying to tell you. Most of the time, associating and not actually listening will negatively influence the development of the conversation. Associating means that while listening, the content of what is being said is related to your past experiences. This principle of connecting verbalised content and memories of personal experiences is based on perceived similarity. These associations are then brought into the conversation, and to really listen is forgotten. As a result, it is getting more and more unlikely somebody is really understood. Often personal ideas and opinions are then being forced upon others. The verbalised content is formed according to these presumptions. Eventually, these are going to be reproduced in a **monologue** and will disturb the process of building or having an actual **dialogue**. These biased, highly personal perspectives are then determined as being his "problem". Probably the answer to the "problem" is also already known and gets presented victoriously. Suppose somebody is tensed up and gets the impression that the counterpart isn't paying any attention to the things he is saying, and the counterpart does not make an effort to try to understand him and the situation-In that case, this is likely to trigger angry hostile reactions. Sometimes these frustrations are being held back, and some people accept being patronised if a solution is hard to find and a way out is being looked for while being put under a lot of verbal pressure. Others are less assertive by nature and tend to comply according to the expectations of others. Notwithstanding, the real problem is not going to be solved by following this path and at some time this theme will emerge again.

My experience showed me that to be able to analyse efficiently and to get the information leading to the underlying motivation, it is necessary to communicate on a factual and rational level and to refrain from formulating messages on a personal level. Open W-questions (what, where, who, why and when) are the most suitable for effective analysis. With this form of questioning the level of self-revelation of your counterpart is being addressed. This provides important and revealing information. I will explain these rhetorical formulas for questions in the following sections.

Intuition

The content of messages is communicated on both a verbal and a nonverbal level. Some messages, however, are being transmitted "below" the surface of what is verbally expressed. This information can also be perceived and interpreted. Some people are not able to express personal needs clearly, especially when they are under the influence of stress and are highly agitated. Also, some people in general lack communicative skills, others are just not aware of their needs and motives or feel blocked, or they are too shy and not self-confident enough.

A large part of the total content is not being expressed on an accessible conscious level but is rather being transmitted subliminally during a conversation. This content can also be "heard" and will (unconsciously) be given a specific meaning depending on the person perceiving it and the context of the situation. This perceived content leads to subtle impressions, feelings, or the formation of mental pictures of what this person is implicitly trying to say but cannot express verbally. These feelings and pictures are principally accessible and potentially valuable for our analysis. However, it is required to objectify the validity of these "mental pictures" and feelings by expressing them to this person. It is not wise to give these personal impressions instant credibility and to interpret them as being valid. This would lead to fixations and probably causes a conversation to end up on a dead-end road.

Interpreting nonverbal signs and signals

Nonverbal communication is formed by internal processes and is influenced by the context and the dynamics of the conversation. With nonverbal communication or body language, meaningful messages are transmitted using mimic, gestures, body signs or other non-verbal ways of expression. These signs are critical sources of information. A large part of our communication takes place via this channel. Nonverbal signs also deliver the most reliable cues. This way of expression is hard to fake and precisely indicates how somebody really feels about a situation.

To gather extra information about the other person and his mindset regarding the situation, attention should regularly be directed towards the nonverbal signs transmitted during the actual communication process. It can also be very helpful to recognise any distinct changes as the negotiation progresses over time. If for some reason, a defensive or offensive position is taken on at the beginning or during the conversation, a pure solution-orientated style of communicating is not going to be effective. Then it makes more sense first to try to positively influence this hostile demeanour by using "disarming" rhetoric.

I often experienced people trying to verbally de-escalate without somebody being open to it. In some cases, this led to unwanted and contra-productive developments concerning the whole situation. In one specific instance, a highly frustrated person felt he was put under even more pressure, boxed in, threatened by a former colleague who tried to verbally intervene because he personally wanted to. This colleague disregarded the state his counterpart was in. It simply was not possible for this person to understand what my colleague wanted from him and to realise that the efforts he made came from the best intentions. In the end, this individual launched a physical attack. On another occasion, the person concerned was in an uncooperative defensive mode from the beginning. The content rebounded on a mental defensive wall. By speaking constantly and trying to find a solution, a lot of energy was eventually lost with achieving little or no result. Also, I experienced a situation in which a tense and completely socially withdrawn person first accepted the solution presented to him while (not deliberately) being put under a lot of pressure. On the other hand, this situation had nothing to do with him personally nor his actual concerns. But then again, did he not protest against it. In this highly complex case, it was tough to get orientation on how to conduct the conversation from the beginning and where it was going because this person neither spoke nor socially interrelated with others at all. The solutions, of course, were not satisfying in the end and did not solve the underlying problem. Maybe this individual gave in because he somehow wanted to escape from the "rhetoric information enforcing" some people tend to demonstrate when they do not get the response they are looking for. Anyhow, in the end, an extremely aggressive (re-)action took place. For the people involved, it was hard to understand the origin of this behaviour. It should be remembered that a lot of aggression results from an accumulation of frustrating experiences and stress. Most of the time, tension builds up progressively over time and with it, anxiety and agitation are going to increase. Often it will be hard to relate the conflict to the aggression itself. In this latter specific situation with the "mute" individual, one must bear in mind that if you try to find a solution by putting a lot of effort into it, you should never completely disregard your personal feelings. It is then better to change your strategy. Constantly trying to support a person not showing any sign of cooperation is at some point going to cause frustration. The risk that you will act emotionally, impulsive and counterproductive is real. Then the situation becomes even more complicated and turbulent, as you probably can imagine.

Another factor that could provide important clues and information about the other person and the progression of the conversation is the **congruence or incongruence between** what has been said and the observed **nonverbal signs and messages**. For example, a person verbally expresses the following sentence: "Yes, this solution will fit for me". However, you observe typical nonverbal signs clearly indicating dissatisfaction and resignation (the look in the eyes, mimic and posture). It is best to orientate yourself to this non-verbal level of communication. Non-verbal body signals are hard to influence and to manipulate consciously. These signs provide valuable clues about the true feelings lying "underneath".

Intuition could also provide clues indicating "something is not right". Your observations of possible discrepancies can be verbalised openly and brought to someone's attention, as long as the tension within this person is not too high and a lot of angriness and hostility is being suppressed. Otherwise, the risk for an escalation is real. You can use a sentence like this: "**I heard (always use the I perspective)** what you told me, but I do have the impression (by the way you express yourself or bodily signs) you are not really/completely satisfied". Verbally mirroring observed behavioural cues is an effective way to raise awareness about real feelings that are somehow (unconsciously) being compensated for or denied. Transparency, for me, is an important basic principle to de-escalate most situations, like being authentic. All in all, by applying these practical, effective techniques, a good constructive base for a further conversation can be achieved

Perceive the transferred information in its entirety

For the individual with whom the conversation takes place, certain specific personal circumstances are always of relevance. The conversation should therefore be based on these meaningful aspects of this individual's personal life. You can only really understand what motivates somebody if you manage to understand what is of importance to him in a certain context. Finding solutions is going to be more accessible, and becoming successful is more likely.

With personal circumstances, I mean all relevant aspects like family, work, home conditions, etc. This valuable information can be registered by listening well, asking open questions, but also by making use of informational resources and your intuition. When you use intuition as a resource, it is important not to underestimate the risk of being biased. In case you are in doubt, make sure to get an objective confirmation regarding your impressions. Such confirmation is acquired by simply reflecting your thoughts and feelings openly and asking for feedback.

The degree to which personal information can be brought into the occasion largely depends on the resources you have at your disposal and the context you're in. In some professional fields of activity like schools, social and medical institutions, there are plenty of ways to get a much more differentiated picture of the person concerned because personal relevant information and documents are actively gathered. With brief interactions, this opportunity won't be available. Under these circumstances, your basic human knowledge, prior experiences and intuition still could prove to be good resources for providing clues.

Theory and practice

Conducting solution-oriented, de-escalating conversations is always a challenge. It all may seem obvious and easy when reading this text. Using these techniques as a practical tool and sticking to the described guidelines will not be easy, especially under the influence of stress. However, real skills come with practice. Theoretical knowledge can only be integrated by going through the process of having practical experiences. Integrated skills make it possible to adapt flexibly to the challenges life is, without a doubt, going to throw at us. Verbal de-escalating techniques are no exception to this rule. Acquiring fundamental skills happens only through a path of trial and error. This path gives us the experiences we need to have to be adequately prepared to deal with these kinds of situations.

A de-escalating conversation is like dancing; both parties play a significant role and depend on each other. Nevertheless, it would be best if you always led this dance.

Step 4: Resolve the conflict with the use of verbal techniques

As soon as you have managed to actively balance out the form of aggression or enough energy has been released by the venting of frustration of the aggressor, and as a result, this individual has calmed down and is able to think again, it is the right moment to take the next step: try to find a solution for the conflict and to get to the underlying motivation of people for showing aggressive behaviour. Sometimes people also leave the scene, and therefore taking this step is not required. In other situations, it is impossible to find a solution because you withdrew yourself or other people like colleagues have taken over the situation and you are no longer actively involved. However, if it is required to find fundamental solutions by using verbal de-escalating techniques, the following important elements should be taken into consideration.

Location, location, location!

It is not always possible to choose under what kind of circumstances a de-escalating conversation will take place. Often, you find yourself being frontally confronted with a challenge like a massive conflict and you won't be able to change the location or look for a suitable room. Then you have to try to make the best out of the situation in the "here and now". Nevertheless, you should be aware of relevant aspects and alter certain requirements if applicable and possible. These could be of real importance and determine whether a conversation is going to be a constructive one and, even more importantly, whether you can stay safe during the process.

The main goal is to arrange quiet surroundings and facilitate the absence of distractive influences and counterproductive stimuli like those coming from curious people, patients, clients, other personnel, etc. Bystanders sometimes impose real challenges and can cause serious problems. They could easily trigger the next escalation and provoke complicated and dangerous responses. Whenever other people interfere, it is a real possibility that out of one tricky situation, suddenly, two separate challenges with multiple participants emerge. Then you will have a hard time managing to stay in control. Aggressive people sometimes make opportunistic use of bystanders. They could be utilised as a type of theatre stage audience, and as a result, the negative dynamics are going to be additionally fed by the attention of others. Even people being around only observing and watching the scene regularly cause massive problems. Aggressive people could feel embarrassed and possibly see no other way out than to act more aggressively to solve this difficult impasse. Hardened positions, a tense standoff or even an escalation are likely to occur.

If you cannot change rooms, at least the distractive and possible harmful bystanders should be asked to leave. Sometimes this can only be achieved by uttering a loud verbal command. In most strained situations, I nearly always had to deal with curious bystanders, who think it is fascinating and thrilling to watch and observe high-intensity situations. It naturally draws a lot of attention, for it means "action" and a welcome distraction from maybe an uneventful, mundane life. Except for the adverse influences, another reason to demand those people to leave: guard the safety of those watching the spectacle.

It is always a good idea to start the conversation by asking your conversational partner **to take a seat**. Sitting is of relevant symbolic importance in social relations, too (for example, sitting at the fireplace and storytelling). Conducting a negotiation while seated will make things much easier on most occasions. It determines and creates a common space for both parties in which it is simpler to stay focused. Also, the way the other person reacts to the question to take a seat is a good indicator of willingness to cooperate and general verbal accessibility. This simple question provides a lot of information you can make use of to read people. In the event this person declines your question and reacts highly defensively, it is a clear sign that it will turn out to be challenging.

A table can be very effective as a barrier between you and an agitated and possibly violent individual. It is important not to take a frontal position to avoid making an overly confrontative, dominant impression. It is preferable to be sitting in an angular position to your counterpart. On most occasions, I wait and observe which seat an individual takes or whether he waits until I ask him to take a seat or point one out. After this initial sequence, I choose my position accordingly. Occasionally, people mostly decide to take the very well recognisable "boss chair" or sit onto a chair very well recognisable for not being available to non-employed individuals (directly behind a running computer) at your workplace. This whole initial phase is a good source for information too.

Suppose these kinds of tense and sometimes complicated and challenging conversations occur regularly because of the context (psychiatric ward, customer and social service, etc.). In that case, it can be a real advantage to organise or buy some lower, softer chairs. These types of chairs make it more difficult for a potentially violent person to launch a sudden physical attack without you being able to respond to it.

A large room is not preferable for having de-escalating talks with agitated people. In a larger room, you will see that people start moving around and not calming down or coming to rest that easily. On the other hand, small rooms are mostly experienced as being too confined. Highly stressed people might feel cramped and pressurised. The most appropriate rooms have a friendly, calm and soothing atmosphere. Objects which can be used to throw at you or others should be removed at all times on these occasions. This also counts for expensive and personal items that could get damaged or destroyed and raise concerns. Especially when this space is used for this purpose more often, these aspects should be considered and adapted, if necessary. A designated place for having conversations would be the most optimal solution. You could design and furnish it for this purpose only. All these important matters can be taken into account without influencing routine procedures negatively. You also prevent that these basic principles are not considered or sometimes even forgotten in the heat of the moment. If this was to happen, it could have dire consequences concerning personal safety.

The **door of the room** where a de-escalating conversation takes place must **always be available and remain unblocked and accessible** to both parties, so nobody feels penned in or becomes trapped. An available exit represents a way out in case of an emergency. People generally experience more pressure, instinctively feel exposed and get anxious whenever a door is blocked or an exit is not available. Blocked doors often lead to an increase in tension, and people are less likely to relax. In the event of trying to de-escalate a situation, you are already going through a tense and challenging process. A door opening to the outside is a real advantage, if not a requirement. It should be kept in mind that a possible hostile aggressor could try to barricade himself in with everyone else in a room. A door that only opens inward and an aggressive person positioning himself right in front of it could quickly make a situation dangerous. Try it for yourself. By only putting your bodyweight to a door and leaning onto it, this will make it almost impossible for somebody else to open the door and get out of this room. Even if you would try with all your strength, it becomes more of a physical struggle and probably a real fight, which, of course, should be avoided at all costs.

It also makes sense to install panic buttons as an extra electronic security measure in specially designated areas and locations. This can be an actual mechanical button placed under a table or on a wall next to you, but it can also be integrated digitally onto your computer to warn other people connected to you in a workplace network. Alarm or panic buttons are important to keep you safe. These measures also will reduce your stress level and make it easier to concentrate and stay focused.

Finding solutions

To make offered solutions work, certain verbal rhetorical techniques can be used to bring the need and motivation "behind" the aggressive behaviour onto a conscious level of this individual. In other words, your counterpart needs to become aware of his motivation for showing this behaviour. It will not help the process if we only "know" or sense what his needs (possibly) are and then try to offer a solution for a "problem" this person himself isn't aware of. A solution serves the problem or needs this person has and therefore has to fit adequately.

In many cases, we might have the (fore-) knowledge or a picture in our mind what kind of problem somebody has or what it is all about. It could be tempting to present solutions or to put them into somebody's mouth, even if this individual is still completely unaware of his personal issues. Especially during a stressful and tense interaction, it would be convenient to find an (easy) way out of this situation. Sometimes this can work out very well. In the long term, however, it is better to clearly define and assess the person's needs. Pictures and guestimates are likely to originate from one's own experiences. The conversational partner could feel patronised in the case where inept solutions are being presented. He may get the impression that he is not being taken seriously. It is more appropriate to go through the complete process, make this person aware of their own needs, and raise conscious awareness of the personal issues with effective, rhetoric guiding techniques.

A ground-laying basis to achieve this awareness is the existence of adequate functioning, cognitive capabilities for the aggressor. The ability to think and reflect becomes progressively impaired as soon as internal pressure increases. So again, one of the rules is to make sure that this individual calms down (by himself) to some extent.

Then we try to establish contact at eye level. This provides a fundamental basis from which it is generally (neurologically) possible to be effective at verbally de-escalating the situation by actively finding a solution for his problem.

Rhetorical tricks and techniques

Conflict and aggressive behaviour are always directly or indirectly triggered by discrepancies concerning personal needs. As I mentioned before, the main goal is that both parties should build an understanding of "what it is all about" and that the somewhat calmed down person should "see" or perceive their own problems and/or dilemma. Based on the understanding of the real issue, you can eventually suggest a solution if needed. Some people express the problem they have and can also find a solution for themselves without our help.

Regarding verbal de-escalating techniques, open type questions principally have the best characteristics to build a relationship, gather useful information, and bring a motive into mind. The following leading/supportive phrases mostly lead to an understanding of the motive very quickly and efficiently:

> - **"What is the issue here?"**
> - **"What is it about?"**
> - **"Can you tell me what it is all about?"**
> - **"I do not understand what it is all about. Could you tell me?"**

This type of questioning knows all in all many variations. It depends on the person and context you are in what will prove to be most suitable. By asking these types of questions, you are suggesting "it" is about "something". This suggestion directly addresses the motivation that is superimposed by conflict or aggressive behaviour. On the other hand, a willingness to support the aggressor is being implicitly transmitted too. An open direct question like this leads typically very rapidly to a constructive dialogue and creates trust. It influences and changes the dynamics from being turbulent and destructive into becoming constructive and solution-oriented. Aggressive people are also caught and kind of lost, feeling anxious and stressed out. In most cases, they aren't aware of what it was all about that made them behave as they did in the first place. It is important to de-emotionalise the dynamics by bringing them to a rational level. After you made this entry in the conversation, you likely got on eye level again. If needed, you can further explore the motivation and needs with sentences starting with the basic pronouns: "Who"; "What"; "When", etc.

I hardly use "Why" as it puts too much pressure on the counterpart into providing an explanation.

However, if someone is excited and emotionally unstable, open questions with the previously mentioned pronouns occasionally lead to a free flow of speech. This is sometimes hard to stop and to get a grip on. Even when people talk a lot on these occasions, the information you really need is still not brought to light. These straining, tedious monologues, therefore, do not lead to the pursued objective. Also, trying to listen carefully and being attentive to these monologues will drain your energy rapidly. In the long term, you will lose attention and interest in the conversation, and even feelings of frustration are likely to occur. In these situations, it is important to get in charge of the conversation to pursue your objectives again. This can be achieved by taking on a more pronounced leading position. It is your task to be aware of, control and adjust your personal attitude as the conversation changes, shifts and develops into different directions. You need to guard the general framework in which this conversation takes place.

The following assertive kind of sentences can be used to get the conversation on track again:

"I heard what you said, but can you please explain to me what this is really all about" or "What is it that you want or need?"

The person should express the actual need. They and not you should verbalise it. When this individual verbally expresses their need, it can be assumed a consciousness is finally gained about the actual "want" and the so-called "what it is about". After this vital step, it is now time for you to find and offer a concrete solution or a compromise which will depend on the context and the individual you are dealing with.

However, even after successfully establishing a balanced basis for a constructive conversation, some partners still need extra rhetoric attention to become aware of their actual needs. This can be achieved by mirroring the hypothetical satisfaction of the demands and by asking about the meaning it would hold. With this kind of rhetorical technique, thinking and reflecting processes are supported. This helps your counterpart to gain consciousness about the actual needs.

Using a sentence like: **"Assuming that you get 'what you want', what will this mean to you?"** has this effect.

Perhaps your counterpart can now interrelate the existing situation but probably wasn't completely aware of their unspecific demands. They then can perceive on a conscious level what it is all about and what the motivations are. This awareness-raising, considering underlying motivations, results from the "complementary effect" of this "as if" projection or presented hypothetical solution.

Or maybe after asking this question, your speaking partner becomes aware that there wasn't any problem at all, to begin with. Maybe this conflict was used as a good reason and an excuse to vent stress and feelings of frustration. In this case, finding solutions makes no sense because there isn't a real problem that can be solved. As you gain more experience in dealing with these kinds of situations, you will recognise scenes like these. With experience, you can more easily change perspectives from being a participant into being an observer. These scenes can be quite interesting to watch, and sometimes people behaving like this can be kind of entertaining, to be honest. People can perform stage-like scenes, in which you might or might not also play a part. These roles are mostly related and limited to a certain professional context and not to be taken too personally.

A very effective variation of the previously mentioned question is:

"If I would grant you this/allow you this (i.e., demand), what difference would it make to you?" or **"What does it mean to you?**

This sentence can bring the actual need into mind too. At the same time, support is being implicitly offered. This is almost always going to lead to constructive development of the conversation.

In some cases, it still might remain unclear and vague what motivations caused the conflict or this person to behave aggressively. For some people, it is not easy to reason for themselves or connect to their problems. If it is necessary to find a solution and actively defuse the situation, contrasting the positive and negative implications can bring the motives to mind. First, you ask what it would mean if the demands **cannot** be satisfied (negative implications). Then, you ask what it would mean if his demands **can** be satisfied (positive implications).

By approaching this matter from two opposite contrasting sides, you raise consciousness concerning personal needs. The positive implication can be used as a "bridge" to propose a possible solution effectively.

> ➢ **What will it mean to you, if you cannot... (demand)?**
> ➢ **What will it mean to you, if you can... (demand)?**

As soon as the needs are expressed, it can be assumed that the person has brought the motivation into mind. At this moment, a proper solution can be presented, or a compromise can be discussed to resolve the conflict. By following this sequence, they will have the opportunity to decide for themselves whether this proposal is suitable, and they are willing to accept it or not.

If the proposal you made triggers objections and resistance, it is necessary to go back a few steps with the analysis. It is then required to try and find out again what the real problem is and where the possible discrepancies between the concerns and the solution you suggested lie. Maybe the other did not understand you correctly because of basic communication problems. Or the information that you provided was misinterpreted, or the situation was misjudged, which caused the discrepancy. Some people also use the situation to act out their frustration, as I pointed out earlier. In the latter case, it is better to take on a passive defensive posture, stay cool, guard yourself mentally, show thick skin, and outlast this emotional outburst, or this person simply leaves the occasion.

The best-case scenario is when the proposed solution solves the problem. In reality, however, you cannot always satisfy the needs of another person 100%. More often, you have to go through the process of negotiating into reaching a kind of compromise of which the outcome ultimately manages to satisfy both parties. This could prove to be challenging and rhetorically more demanding. Your counterpart has to step down from his initial demands as the needs will merely be partly met. On the other hand, you should stay aware that it is undoable and often counterproductive to always comply with the demands of somebody else. It is inevitable to push for a compromise if you have the impression that cooperation without any predetermined conditions would lead to discrepancies concerning your own needs and professional tasks. If you structurally try to avoid conflicts by being non-reflective in acting cooperative, this will, in the end, create more problems than you bargained for.

In a lot of discussions, it will be important to firmly represent your boundaries **and** transmit a principal willingness to support simultaneously. On the one hand, the triggering of unnecessary frustrations in this stage of negotiating with people is prevented compared to taking a purely inflexible, self-oriented position. On the other hand, by representing and defining boundaries, you can get on eye level in the relationship, and it has a stabilising effect on an unstable individual (so-called "structuring" by representing a helping "I" or ego). This lies in comparison to being "fuzzy" and acting ambiguous about what can be expected and where and when lines will be drawn. Being fuzzy and always going along like a chameleon makes it hard to be respected as others cannot perceive your boundaries. By defining limitations concerning your capabilities to cooperate and provide support, you represent a counterpart that should be taken seriously and respected. Respecting someone is being aware of this person and taking this person's needs into account.

Another important aspect of being clear and definite about possibilities and limitations is the prevention of so-called "precedents", which are likely to cause difficulties in future situations. The problem with an expressed precedent ("Yesterday your colleague allowed me to…"; "I was allowed to do this before…") is that it is rhetorically representing a direct expectation or even a demand you should comply with the demands because another person (co-worker for example) supposedly granted them before on another occasion. It is more or less a question or demand, transferring a pretended subjective right to get what is asked for. These precedents mainly originate from past situations in which other people were indeterminate in their positions concerning possibilities and limitations. Due to the implicit meaning of precedents, they leave the impression there is hardly any room to contemplate whether you want to cooperate or not. You must oblige, or else… Nevertheless, by being definite and clear, and in case you are part of a team by acting consistently, precedents can be prevented.

By aiming for a compromise with your negotiating techniques, you will come to know whether this person intends to satisfy his needs aggressively or is willing to change his behaviour and become more cooperative. People who remain aggressive and do not show any respect concerning your boundaries and needs can be confronted by taking on a defensive position to try to influence their attitude to become more constructive and get on eye level again.

If, however, a situation threatens to escalate and it is not possible to direct and deflect destructive dynamics, or if it doesn't make any sense to put a lot of energy into trying to influence the conversation, it can be a better option to avoid a frontal confrontation by going along and behaving like a piece of bamboo in the wind. This means that this person finds his demands being met, or you completely withdraw yourself from the situation (physically).

Also, expressing an offensive warning should be considered as an option. It could also help to influence the dynamics, but the effects will depend on the circumstances under which you use these offensive gestures.

To issue a warning; the sometimes-inevitable bending or breaking.

A warning has its place in case a constructive approach is impossible, or it is foreseen that the dynamics will escalate. Issuing a warning is much different in comparison to threatening somebody. Threats are transmitted on a purely personal (offensive) level. Threatening someone tends to influence the highly tense circumstances negatively. It all becomes too personal, and people feel attacked. An expressed warning has a factual character. Warnings illustrate what the logical consequences are going to be if a more constructive path on eye level into reaching a solution or compromise is not chosen.

Examples:

> **Warning on a personal level; "If you do not comply with these requirements, I will…"**
> **Warning on a factual level: "I have to warn you that if you do not comply with these requirements, this will lead to these consequences**".

Before issuing a warning, it is important to ensure that the expressed consequences can be carried out if the referred requirements are not being met. Otherwise, all credibility and probably the general control over the situation will be lost. To stay in control after it becomes evident you are not able to live up to your warnings is going to cost a lot of effort. This means that your energetic resources will be drained eventually. It is even possible you might lose control altogether and cannot regain it. Trying to get back in control could easily cause situations to escalate.

An already aggressive and agitated person probably does not want to give up his control and power and will react frustrated and feel overly challenged if you attempt to force him back.

An issued warning gains weight and extra meaning whenever you create a vivid mental picture by verbally illustrating the consequences or by concretely demonstrating you are serious about carrying through with your demands. Concretising a warning and establishing power to enforce a more cooperative attitude can be achieved by using additional staff and even getting the police or security personnel involved. Sometimes it could also be very effective to open the exit door and demand this person to leave if they choose not to comply with your demands or isn't willing to discuss this matter constructively and decently, like inside a club or waiting room. It depends on the circumstances and the person you are dealing with when deciding on practical measures and what should be expressed to be the most effective. However, the basic principle is always the same: to point out boundaries and define what is acceptable and what is not.

If you decide to issue a warning, it is a good option to rhetorically build in a so-called "golden bridge". People tend to get themselves into difficult situations, and at some time, they probably start to feel they would lose their face if they would give in to our warnings. Giving in is likely to be regarded as something hurtful to their ego, and they probably would feel ashamed as a result. This is likely to happen when other people are around, watching and observing. Due to these instinctive human mechanisms, you will find people persist in resisting our efforts and staying in control to prevent losing their face. People could even get more aggressive instead of complying with our demands whenever they find themselves in this kind of dilemma. My experience says, in situations where people have the option between acting out aggressively or dealing with feelings of shame, most choose the first alternative, even when it is a very destructive way to try to save oneself from feeling ashamed. This dilemma ("When I give in or become more compliant, I will lose my face in this crowd.") represents a kind of "frustration trap" out of which this person cannot really escape by any good means. If you (unintentionally) apply more pressure and corner people dealing internally with these kinds of dilemmas, you could create a dangerous situation.

Therefore, you must always try to build in and to leave open a "golden bridge", "backdoor", or "stage exit". A person who feels cornered can use this opportunity to get out of the trap without losing their face. The rhetoric formula to achieve this effect is "I have to warn you, if you do not do A, this will mean B (implication), but you can also…" (This is the actual "backdoor"). When somebody chooses to use this golden bridge, you can confirm they made the right choice by making positive gestures. This is also a good strategy to lead this individual over the bridge and prevent him from changing his mind.

Make him be the specialist for his problems.

In some cases, negotiation is long, tedious and troublesome, and does not actually lead to the targeted objective, which is, of course, finding a solution and therefore de-escalating the situation. People occasionally discuss and talk all the time without ever getting to the point. Your position could become the main topic of the discussion, perhaps putting you to the test too. The conversation will tend to drift away from the central theme by this seemingly endless discussion. This can be frustrating, as you are trying to lead a conversation with a particular goal in mind. But there is a way out of this straining entanglement; just let this person become the specialist who can solve their own problems! Then you disrupt most unproductive discussions and power struggles. This little rhetoric technique allows you to cut yourself loose, get back in control again, and by doing so, the effects of stress are regulated, and feelings of frustration are compensated. Making him be his own specialist means that this person is asked upfront what they would do or what solution they think of as best and appropriate if they were in our position. As a result of this type of questioning, this conversational partner is rhetorically made to think about their position in relation to ours, putting the said person into proper perspective again. By using these kinds of rhetoric tricks, you'll find discussions instantly stop being unproductive, people are going to calm down, they can orientate themselves better, and you can lead the discussion again at some point.

However, this technique should not be used in case the tension level is already very high. Likely, highly agitated people cannot deal with these kinds of rhetoric twists and turns. An aggressive reaction could be triggered easily when people feel over-challenged by our questions that demand that they change perspectives and reflect. It could be the last straw that breaks the camel's back.

Trust your gut feelings or intuition into judging the suitability before you decide to use this rhetoric intervention.

Depersonalising the conversation

A dialogue could end up getting too personal. Fact is that it will be challenging to find a solution on this basis. By referring to higher entities, you lead the fixated attention of the discussion partner away, enabling you to bring the conversation on a factual level again.

As a person in a professional context, your tasks are representative of abstract professional structures and goals of an organisation or institution. Because of the implicit meanings these representations have for others, they can easily be the reason for conflict, and people behave aggressively and frustrated towards you. This means you are attackable on a personal level, even when you are executing a professional duty. These kinds of conflicts based on projections are strenuous and sometimes hard to solve. Personal feelings and professional tasks easily get mixed up. Over time you probably lose oversight, and you find yourself getting more and more personally entangled in these dynamics. It is not hard to imagine what this will mean for your stress level and how this will eventually lead to feelings of frustration. Due to rising tension levels and the emotions triggered, these situations could easily cause impulsive responses on your behalf. Whenever you remind yourself of the fact you are "only" doing your job and it is not the private "you" that is being addressed if people demand, insult, and exert pressure on you, this will help mentally guard yourself.

Personally, I regularly (almost in a mantra-like manner because I often deal with conflict and aggression, and it is not always easy to distinguish that I am actually at work, as I am wearing regular clothes) verbalise the fact that I am only doing my job, and not fulfilling my personal needs. I even describe my function at my workplace and its implicit possibilities and limitations in a very explicit way and refer to the higher entities I am working for. These "entities" determine what I have to ask and sometimes demand from people professionally and not me personally, as a private person ("I am working here, these are the rules applied in this building which my bosses are determining and I have to see that they are being met").

114

Organisational structures are too abstract for most people, especially in the event they cannot think straight anymore. By referring to these abstract "objects", you lead the attention away from yourself into a kind of "void" in which it is hard for somebody to find "something" to project his anger onto. With a combination of these mental and practical elements, you can very effectively depersonalise and defuse turbulent unsatisfying dynamics. Most individuals simply comply or leave the situation.

After variations of rhetorical phrases have been creatively implemented during a verbal de-escalating intervention, you probably managed to change the discussion from being frontal, tense and difficult, into being more constructive and solution-oriented. Interactions could also come to an end quite suddenly when people decide to just walk away. In those cases, it is not required to succeed and put effort into finding a proper solution. This is quite normal, even if it might feel unsatisfying if a process suddenly comes to a halt. It is a part of the deal when attempting to solve challenging situations on a regular basis. Another chance to try again will most certainly occur, and new inter-human conflicts lie there waiting for you in the future, especially when working and dealing with people, for example, in social and service-oriented professions.

The next step

Processing your experiences with conflict and aggression and even conducting a debriefing is the next step to take. Debriefings can be organised in many ways, and they are more important than people tend to realise. Debriefings make it possible to review (personal) experiences, relieve ourselves from pent-up emotions, and let off stress. How the debriefing process will pan out depends on the context and the degree to which people feel affected. These factors also determine implicitly what organisational and timely resources are needed to debrief such occurrences properly.

It could be an option to debrief extraordinary stresses and strains with colleagues mandatorily. This would allow the people negatively affected by aggression to regain a professional attitude and to stay healthy over the long term. The effects of debriefings also imply the regaining of inner stability and sometimes even preventing burnout syndromes. To relieve ourselves from stresses and strains and negative thoughts, feelings and impressions, it could be sufficient to express these personal experiences to someone we trust and have a relationship with. These psycho-hygienic conversations are commonly practised automatically with friends or family in our private surroundings without most people being aware of the deeper meaning.

However, in case we have to deal with aggression professionally on a regular basis, it sometimes takes more than to only relieve ourselves shortly from intense impressions. Then it is also important to reflect on (re-)actions to aggressive behaviour critically and then come to conclusions about which approaches can be improved. In many psychosocial institutions, this counts even more because negative experiences of employees could have far-reaching consequences for the clients, mainly depending on the same professionals and their actions.

Step 1: Regulate acute stress

| Step 2: Identify the form of aggression | | Find a suitable location and offer a seat |

| Step 3: Adapt by adjusting your attitude | | Direct the attention away from the conflict and aggression |

| **Step 4:** Apply negotiation techniques after balancing out the aggression | | Apply rhetoric tricks to efficiently find a solution |

Issue a warning if nessecary, to get the conversation on track again

Consider making him the specialist to his own problems

Depersonalize the dialogue if it gets to personal

Step 5: The debriefing

In professional areas, where people structurally have to cope with extraordinary burdensome and straining challenges like the police, the fire department and emergency medical services, it is in many cases common to debrief these experiences with all the people involved. On some occasions, even additional help of external professional resources like psychologists, supervisors and other specially trained people is also necessary to assist in the debriefing process. Debriefings are held for good reasons. The main goal is to accelerate the adequate processing of stressful experiences and prevent mental problems.

In other areas, for example, in schools, hospitals, social communities, departments of justice and security organisations, debriefings are not always offered. Working in these professional areas means being structurally exposed to high demands and challenging situations, like dealing with aggression. These experiences can and will, on a lot of occasions, leave temporary and sometimes lasting marks. It is not hard to imagine the importance, if not the professional necessity, to organise debriefings in these areas too.

Most employees coming from these professions express a need for regular or at least occasional debriefings. The people on the working floor - those confronted and exposed to aggression – all recognise this necessity. Sometimes the thinking of leaders in specific areas needs to shift. They should do some serious contemplating about their general priority settings and make decisions to provide a decent organisation for the necessary organisational structures for conducting debriefings and care for the mental health of their employees.

Confrontations with aggression (highly frustrated people, acts of physical violence, provocations and intimidations), and the requirement to deal with this destructive behaviour professionally put a lot of pressure on all people involved. Sometimes the after-effects are too much to deal with, and if left unprocessed, they could cause lasting negative effects. Just these facts alone should usually be convincing and motivating enough for organisations to implement debriefings. Debriefings also help to prevent future occurrences from being affected by prior negative experiences in a counterproductive way.

They prevent a possible strong subjective priming of referential models. This possible negative effect due to an unprocessed exposure to challenging, burdensome, and sometimes even traumatising occurrences could make it more difficult to assess future occasions without being heavily biased (possibly causing overreactions). The applied interventions can be reviewed during a debriefing, and thoughts about the improvement of general strategies can be made.

Processing demanding experiences

It is sometimes difficult to effectively process and digest experiences that leave massive impressions without any help from others. This is because the ability to perceive past occurrences and the means to reflect are naturally limited to one's perspective. All people have natural blind spots regarding their personality traits and behavioural tendencies. These aspects remain blind and inaccessible as long as you do not receive any feedback from others. Suppose you would decide to process experiences on your own. In that case, these aspects of other non-accessible levels of your personality cannot be considered and attended to, even though they probably would be relevant for building a broader perspective concerning past occurrences. By trying to digest without the help and input of others, possible offensive or defensive (re-) actions on your behalf cannot easily be perceived in a rational perspective. Therefore, feelings of guilt are likely to occur at some point, even when they are successfully ignored and suppressed at first. This kind of emotional "overreacting" is always a possibility. We are personally affected and will not always manage to compose ourselves and behave professionally.

Another aspect is that generally, as time goes by, most negative impressions shift into the background of our consciousness. New occurrences are going to happen as time goes by, and more recent situations superimpose past unprocessed and undigested burdensome events lingering around in your mind, "waiting" to be attended to. For the reflecting and mirroring of these kinds of experiences and, therefore, being able to work though the negative impressions that, for example, aggressive people leave behind, it is helpful to use suitable counterparts like other persons who were present, but also outsiders you trust and are open to you. These people could also help (sometimes by demanding these debriefings) in generating a meaning to these disturbing situations and animate us to process them. As a result, closure can be found.

Difficult events and experiences which will leave temporary marks no matter how long you are in the job and how proficient you are can be integrated. Remember, feeling stressed, burdened and emotionally charged after dealing with violent forms of aggression is a normal reaction to abnormal occurrences. This has to do with the nature of aggression and its impacts on your system. However, (claiming) not to have any residual feelings at all could be an indicative sign for not being completely honest to yourself and/or towards others, or to the numbing of feelings, (structural) defensive mechanisms, disowned tendencies to offensive (sadistic) aggression and even symptoms of a possible burnout syndrome.

The adequate processing of straining events is greatly beneficial for future occasions because humans mainly learn by doing. Digested and processed experiences provide you with hard-earned additional skills to deal with conflict and aggression. Debriefings are further suitable for expressing and exchanging the thoughts behind executed personal procedures and gaining insight into how they were perceived and valued by other involved people. By discussing and sharing points of view without being judgemental, ambiguities can be balanced out, questions can be asked and (latent) conflicts, which could affect team dynamics negatively, can be solved at an early stage. Remind yourself of this important, often overseen aspect: a balanced team is vital for all members to feel secure and deal with future challenges. It helps prevent conflict and aggression, as people can easily sense whether a team is united or divided. A united team offers a structure for orientation and, therefore, security. People generally feel less secure with a divided team, and some also use this space to play their negative (manipulative) games.

Saving the integrity of mental models

Being left alone with impressions after you had an intense confrontation with destructive behaviour could lead to negative imprinting of the long-term memory. This kind of "negative priming" can become a problem for dealing with actual situations. It could lead to the superimposing of existing, more objective (professional) models of the same subject matter. The qualities of referential models are important. They will influence our assessments of situations, our responses and interventions, and further development of the dynamics. It cannot be prevented that we will be affected by strong experiences. However, it can be prevented that referential models get primed negatively by properly processing these impressions.

Personal experiences determine for a large part the quality of assessments of future occurrences. But also, competencies and skills to deal with actual situations depend on our encounters and lessons learned. This is why it is important to remain critical about how we have dealt with situations. Especially in certain professions, it is necessary to evaluate and reflect on the procedures followed, with all the people involved. This has to take place on non-judgmental and value-free premises. By doing so, we could evaluate which interventions had a positive effect and what wasn't effective or might have been counterproductive. This will benefit insights into what needs to be improved for the next situation to come (maybe even with the same client).

Regarding dealing with aggressive behaviour and in general, whenever an effort is made to manage a wide range of challenging situations professionally, it is seldom beneficial to base the outcome of evaluations on undifferentiated criteria like "wrong" and "right". To discuss on the premises that somebody is personally to blame in case things did not pan out according to the expectations is seldom going to generate any value other than some people (those who were not to blame, of course) might find some peace of mind personally. The whole blaming game is of no real use on a professional working level. Debriefings should be held on a rational basis. This helps to change professional procedures and to gain to new insights and ways to prevent future similar situations ("How did I deal with this situation?"; "What can I do differently in the future?"). By collectively discussing and reviewing experiences, it is prevented that people try to process them on their own and hence start generating negative opinions and feelings of guilt concerning their actions. It can be avoided that they behave insecurely in situations to come and therefore would act less effectively and even exert counterproductive and hazardous influences on borderline dynamics.

Professional debriefings need a basic framework.

It would be ideal to debrief and process encounters with aggressive and violent people as soon as possible after the incident occurred. Waiting too long usually leads to suppression of unprocessed and undigested experiences. They are likely to be superimposed by more recent occurrences. Also, our attention is probably going to be drawn by other stimuli and happenings in our surroundings. The motivation to sit down, talk and debrief declines as time proceeds. No conscious relatedness to what happened usually means; "It is not there anymore, so why to bother talk about it". However, although not clearly present in our conscious awareness, these strong impressions could remain in our system for long periods of time accompanied by many questions, ambiguities, and feelings of guilt, doubt, anger and especially stress, if left unresolved. These residual leftovers can have massive negative impacts on peoples' lives. Leaving strong impressions unprocessed makes them indirectly noticeable due to physical and psychological symptoms or by negatively affecting social lives. The effects could even lead to an inability to work (burnout syndrome).

This is one of the main reasons why it is recommendable to assign a person responsible for the organisation and coordination of debriefings. In most (larger) institutions, designated coordinating or leading functionaries normally organising special interventions or structurally dealing with personal matters are already existent. These officials could easily organise and even should demand that these important debriefings are being held, if necessary.

Some people express concerns that these debriefings or "discussions" will lead to conflicts, personal accusations, and situations in which people might feel insulted and be upset as soon as personal opinions are expressed. These possible issues do not compose the essence of this kind of dialogue, but to be honest, it can neither be prevented nor ruled out. On the other hand, emotional discussions could also provide some necessary "psycho-hygiene". It is, however, possible to facilitate general beneficial conditions and a neutral character for the conversation. For this, a specially printed form can be implemented and used. This provides an overview over the necessary content, and it outlines a logical structure for the debriefing. This form represents the impersonal basis for the conversation, and therefore the individuals involved are not going to determine and influence form and structure too much. It specifies and determines the topics that should be discussed and thematised and doesn't refer to person "A" or "B" personally. By using such a form, debriefings become more neutral and factual and less personal in character.

Interpersonal discrepancies can be acknowledged but should be processed later under more suitable circumstances with or without a mediator being present. A printed form can also evaluate procedures and is implicitly designed to repeat specific topics relevant to understanding aggressive dynamics. It could also be used to share experiences with those colleagues who were not involved but are nevertheless interested in the information and maybe can learn and gain from it.

Elements that can be put onto a printed form and can be helpful are:

> Time/Date/Place
> The names of all persons involved
> Called in external instances and support, like police or security guards
> Describe the event which triggered the aggression
> Were any preliminary signs detected before it came to an aggressive outburst? (Withdrawal, confusion, restlessness, signs of stress, agitation, expressed threats, general hostility, and the damaging of property)
> Describe the interventions that were used to de-escalate the situation. (Verbal negotiation, distraction, tension regulation)
> Did anyone get physically hurt?
> Did anyone involved suffer from psychological/emotional violence?
> Did all persons involved attend the debriefing?

Summary

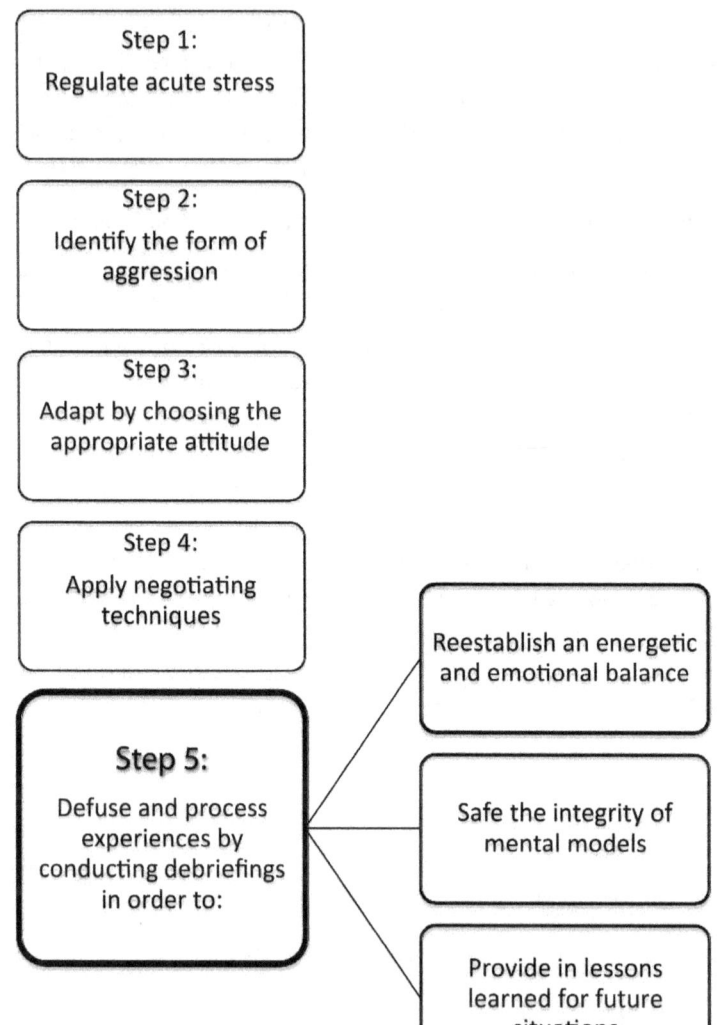

Step 1:

Regulate acute stress

Step 2:

Identify the form of aggression

Step 3:

Adapt by choosing the appropriate attitude

Step 4:

Apply negotiating techniques

Step 5:

Defuse and process experiences by conducting debriefings in order to:

Reestablish an energetic and emotional balance

Safe the integrity of mental models

Provide in lessons learned for future situations

6. Practical examples

The following practical examples demonstrate the five practical steps to de-escalate aggression and resolve conflict (stress regulation, recognising the form of aggression, posture, conversational techniques and debriefing).

Daily routine

I am watching my rear mirror while driving my car on a 2-lane highway, and amid the process of overtaking a truck, I observe a car closing in very fast from behind me. The driver does not appear to slow down, by my estimation. On the contrary, he moves at high speed into close proximity until only two meters are left between my rear bumper and the front of his car. The driver repeatedly starts signalling with his headlights and closes in some more. I feel the pressure rising inside of my body caused by this situation, and my normal breathing stops. I take a few deep breaths, manage to compose myself and complete my overtaking manoeuvre until I can switch lanes (**stress regulation**). With full throttle, the driver instantly overtakes me. I feel angry because of this situation, and my tension increases even more. I start looking for other "irritating" drivers onto whom I can project my anger. In a flash, I suddenly realise how passing on my anger would make things worse. I again take a few deep breaths and then breathe normally. I count from 10 to 1, as I am used to doing (**stress regulation**). My pressure dropped, and I reflected on what happened and how I reacted. "Maybe it was an emergency, and this is why this individual was actually in a hurry", I thought. I will never know.

Alcohol can make things complicated.

Late at night, the train I am travelling on comes to a halt at the station in the small town where I live. "Finally, I am at home after a long day's work. I am tired", I think to myself and leave the train. While walking on the station platform in the direction of the exit, I can hear the distinct loud noise of an older male person talking very loudly, ranting and grumbling in a very "aggressive" manner. According to my prior experiences on this platform, my quick assessment is that it probably is one of the people I met on some prior occasions who are intoxicated from alcohol and hang around, causing disturbances regularly. I know there will be a real potential risk for provocations, and it likely will be a generally troublesome encounter. On my way towards the exit, I come closer to the "intoxicated" elderly person. "Great, he has positioned himself exactly near the stairs, and I need to go past him to leave the station", I think. "I cannot avoid going there, but I won't give him a reason to talk to me, and I must go right past him without showing any signs of uncertainty" is my immediate plan of strategy. I automatically take a deep breath **(stress regulation)** and move on in the direction of the exit. At about a distance of two meters, I observe the highly agitated individual from the corner of my eye. I try to compose myself. However, internally I also simulate other options and prepare myself to deal with an almost inevitable contact. The older, clearly heavily intoxicated man watches me shortly and instantly tries to provoke me by making some remarks about my person **(form of aggression: provocation)**. At the same time, he starts moving towards me. "He will come too close for comfort, that is for sure now", I instantly realise. "This is going to be a difficult and possibly dangerous situation." I turn around until I face the man still closing in on me while automatically breathing deeply **(stress regulation)**. I take in a upright, self-confident position and make a distinct "stop" signal with the palms of my hands **(adapting my attitude: offensive, third level intervention)**. I verbally <u>demand</u> this person to keep a distance from me without paying too much attention to him. The hostile individual stops moving towards me and seems to be distracted by my actions. He responds by ranting furiously and making all sorts of aggressive, offensive pointing gestures with his hands. He nevertheless seems affected and keeps his distance. I know he tries to intimidate me **(form of aggression: provocation)**, but I do not react and remain composed, even when the pressure internally increases to high levels **(stress regulation)**. I remain fairly passive in my opposition and clearly signal my boundaries nonverbally and at what distance I want him to stay **(second level intervention)**. After a few seconds, I notice him moving away from me while shouting and making more insulting remarks. I decide to move on without paying too much attention to this ranting man, go down the stairs and turn my head around a few times to see if he is following me **(adapting my attitude: withdrawing)**. Then I can finally leave the station, get into my car and drive home. While driving, I notice the adrenalin in my system and affecting me: my mouth is dry, I feel tensed up, hyper-alert, highly energised, and I realise I am driving too fast. I think about the scene at the station. Phantasies of what could have happened (a violent attack) and how I could have reacted if I had been attacked (defend myself, run or were other people at the scene?) race through my mind. At home, I still feel stressed. It takes some time, but after taking a shower, putting on some other clothes and taking a seat in my living room, I notice a kind of internal urge to express the prior events at the station to my partner. The pictures in my mind and thoughts about the situation settle down while I tell what had happened and I start to calm down (**stress regulation**). "How was your day", I then ask.

Bending, breaking, or is it better to distract?

I remember how back in the days when I was still working as a security person in a dance club, a highly tensed and agitated individual was standing right in front of me, causing a very threatening situation. He had been expelled from the dance club by my colleagues earlier that evening, but now he felt an injustice had been done to him and he had been treated unfairly. His opinion was that, in reality, there had not been any reason for him to get expelled. He offensively demanded admittance, and he more or less ordered to be allowed to get back in the club to his friends. In a self-confident and arrogating manner, he explained that another security had claimed he "head-butted" some other club-goer, and this was the reason he got expelled, but actually, he had only made a head-butt-like gesture and did not actually hit somebody. "If I had wanted to hit this person, this would have been no problem at all", he said to me with a cocky, arrogant smirk on his face. He was not willing to accept my arguments that his actions are generally not tolerated in this club. This young man did not listen at all and applied even more pressure onto me, constantly repeating his demands (**form of aggression: demanding behaviour**). He also demanded the responsible security employee come out and wanted him to justify his actions or wrongdoing. This individual appeared to become more and more self-confident and offensive with his attitude. He seemed fixated, and he was very tensed up, but he nevertheless controlled himself. I felt very unconformable in this situation and sensed the pressure rising. His explanations for what he did and what he was capable of and his general attitude told me that he knew exactly what he was doing. There were good indications for his access to the use of physical violence (**form of aggression: intimidation, possible intentional violence**). Also, this individual was not accessible for a constructive dialogue, and he could not change perspectives at all. I did not know how to get out of this situation. By going along (**adapting my attitude**), distracting and subtly ignoring him for a while, I was able to gain some time and hoped for a strategy to appear to me or that the situation would change for the better by itself, somehow. Instead, he got more agitated, restless and occasionally very offensive with his gestures, which were now directed to me personally, because he was not getting out of me what he wanted. I had the impression that this situation could escalate quickly, and the risk of physical violence was real (**form of aggression: imminent intentional violence**). If I had offensively demanded him to leave and/or called for more support, I could easily have triggered an escalation and could have caused the situation to spiral out of control in front of all these other people watching the scene while fueling the dynamics by making provocative remarks (**form of aggression: provocation to start a fight**). In a final effort, I decided to act and not to wait any longer. I assertively took him a bit to the side, where he was no longer in the midst of the attention (**adapting my attitude: leading/supportive**). There, I switched roles, and I explained to him in a self-confident, somewhat neutral, rational, "fatherly" way that who exactly expelled him from the club was irrelevant (**using rhetoric techniques**). Whatever is tolerated or not is defined by the management and not by the security personal. "We are only doing our job, can't you see!"; "These are the rules in this club; you must understand this", I told him (**second level intervention: setting boundaries**). He listened to me, seemed irritated but also disorientated because I deflected his focus of attack and brought the discussion to a different level. He then moved away from me. After standing at a distance for a few minutes, he shouted that he would never go to this club again, nor his friends, and repeated all kind of typical insults, not directed at me personally, but in general. Nevertheless, slowly but surely, he left the scene.

An explosive outburst

While working as a nurse in a residential community with juveniles, a fourteen-year-old casually tells me that he is going outside in the evening. I tell him that this isn't allowed anymore because it is already too late to leave the house. The rules in this community principally determine it is not permitted for juveniles younger than 15 years of age to go outside past nine o'clock in the evening. As a follow-up, I wanted to ask why it was so important for him to go outside at this time of day, but it never came this far. The juvenile instantly reacted in a highly agitated manner and turned aggressive towards me. He suddenly walked away, made some remarks in my direction, entered his room and slammed his door shut (**form of aggression: act of frustration**). This situation completely caught me by surprise, and I felt the tension rising in my body. I took a breath and tried to compose myself. I waited and tried not to react immediately, even when I felt the urge to instantly follow him into his room (**stress regulation**). Instead, I positioned myself next to his door. There I could hear him rant and shout inside of his room. I did not have the impression that he had completely lost control over himself, neither did I ever experience this happening before when dealing with this juvenile, so there was no need for immediate action (**I stay centred: neutral position**). I waited a few minutes. I then slowly opened the door and observed him throwing around little insignificant objects like paperwork, schoolwork, and pictures. I still remained aware that this situation could change rapidly for the worse and also, I did not want anything thrown at me. He did not seem affected and showed no reaction to my presence (**first level intervention**). I opened the door some more and took a position inside his room near the doorway, a bit on the side to not block the way out for him but also for me to have an exit available. The room was filled with "aggressive" energy, and I sensed a highly emotional "disturbed" atmosphere. As I am used to these situations and know what helps me to stay composed, I automatically took another deep breath and calmly concentrated on my breathing pattern (**stress regulation**). I tried not to become affected by the energy in this room. I managed to stay calm and attentive and consciously took in a low-profile stance. I waited without speaking a word and observed this young man. After a few minutes, he started calming down a bit and sat on his bed with his head in his hands. I could sense anger, but now also sadness and desperation within him. I calmly told him that I am there in case he might need something (**adapting my attitude: leading/supportive**). He reacted in an angry, hostile way: "You always (the employees) make my life miserable". I stayed calm and again breathed deeply (**stress regulation**). By watching his posture, I noticed his tension slowly but steadily dropping and he appeared more sad than angry. I could carefully approach him now. I carefully asked him to tell me what it was all about. He started sobbing and explained to me that he wanted to go outside, because his girlfriend broke up with him. He wanted to think about the situation alone, as he is used to. We talked some more, and after a while, he calmed down some more, and after drinking some water, he decided to go to sleep. Later at night, I discussed this situation with my colleagues. We decided to adapt our plan and let this patient go out in similar cases in the future as long as he is in decent shape and can promise not to hurt himself or others. I then wrote my usual report.

7. About physical self-defensive measures

Violent people leave us no other choice than to secure ourselves, even with the use of self-defensive countermeasures. The term *self-defence,* however, is not always perceived as something positive but generally as something negative. Especially in social work, there seems to be a contradiction between the professional tasks, general working morals and this specific theme, often resulting in an undifferentiated negative connotation. Self-defensive measures are more or less only associated with physical violence, injuries and adverse effects, considering the retaining of personal integrity, dignity and the appreciation of other people. These rejections, objections and personal resistances may seem totally righteous, and the negative arguments will be true occasionally. On the other hand, to be able to build a differentiated opinion and conclude whether it is improper and inadmissible to use self-defensive techniques, I think the following relevant aspects need to be contemplated and should not be overlooked:

- ➤ Who is going to apply these techniques? (Mindset, personality traits, gender, age, capabilities, skills and understanding of morals)
- ➤ What is considered being used for self-defence? (Specific methods, "schools")
- ➤ Under what kind of circumstances are these self-defensive techniques used? (On the "street" or in a professional context)
- ➤ Against whom? (Male, female, the elderly, kids, and juveniles)
- ➤ And against what? (Form of aggression, the danger level of the attack).

Some other aspects may be considered too. These aspects normally nuance the often one-sided associations and put them into perspective again. It may seem like a paradox, but when you think about it, you will conclude that except for practically being able to defend yourself physically, the principle of self-defence has a high symbolic positive value for many people. The symbolic aspect regarding self-defence has a prophylactic influence on challenging dynamics with (potentially) aggressive people. It also helps to build a foundation for the respect of people showing demanding and difficult behaviour. To feel empowered by principally being able to secure oneself with self-defensive skills enables the balancing of aggression and benefits assertive and appropriate reactions if personal boundaries are being crossed. What I mean is that whenever the (theoretical) capability to react defensively with the proper practical skills exist, this will have an enormously positive effect regarding feeling anxious and experiencing fear and stress. People subjectively feel more secure and show more self-esteem when they are principally able to defend themselves in case there is a potential danger of being attacked. This I call the "I can do this-effect" or belief in self-efficacy. Self-defensive skills fill a "void" people often experience on an individual security level. These capabilities have positive effects; in the event, we are dealing with aggressive people and the risk level (mostly unconscious, individual representations of what is secure or not) increases, and the feeling of security is negatively affected.

Because of the impacts aggression has on most people (it is generally perceived as a distinct unfavourable occurrence), primitive psycho-emotional mechanisms trigger a stress reaction or a so-called "fight-or-flight reaction". The severity of this internal reaction and whether the instinctive impulses can be controlled or not will largely depend on the result of a comparison between the subjectively perceived situation and the individual means to deal or cope with the challenges at hand. Lacking or deficient strategies to handle aggressive occurrences amplify the perceived unfavourable meaning and negative implications. Our fear and stress levels are directly influenced by the availability or absence of skills and capabilities to cope with difficult and straining occurrences. The potency of practical skills, in short, coping strategies to theoretically ward off physical attacks, is gigantic. The way people change their physical stance and behave differently whenever they feel more secure and self-confident is impressive. I experienced this effect very often during my training and seminars. It is a fundamental principle to be able to de-escalate and, with a bit more training, also stay safe on a physical level.

In general, I differentiate between two types of physical aggression: unwanted physical contact due to impulsivity (holding a hand or arm firmly, "bear hugging") and an actual or directed attempt of physical violence (chokehold, pulling hairs, sexual assaults, etc.) When people "only" get physical and, for example, impulsively grab a hand, it is not necessary to react by making overly hostile reactions and certainly not by applying damaging physical violence. These impulsive actions can be solved sparingly and purely defensively without getting violent or hectic and provoking more severe reactions. Remind yourself of the fact that "action always means reaction". Acting too strongly "solely" based on the fact that somebody grabbed your hand or appeared to be dangerous would probably provoke a strong offensive reaction.

By reading this text, attentive readers will notice that confrontations with aggression are more or less part of the job in the areas I work. Like in psychiatric hospitals and social institutions, people sometimes tend to behave differently and impulsively because of the nature of their (psychiatric and social) deficits and disorders. Reacting with excessive force under these contextual circumstances would be inappropriate. It would make working with these people almost impossible, as it damages the necessary relations based on trust.

In my opinion, it should always be the primary goal to compensate for unwanted behaviour by merely doing what is required, no more and no less. This implies the necessity to provide security by assertively repelling a physical attack with effective defensive (or counteroffensive) countermeasures without getting into a real fight. Another dimension concerning self-defence arises when dealing with intentional physical violence. This form of aggression requires a different approach, often beyond the capabilities of most people. Suffering from a chokehold, for example, is a tremendously violent act and is extremely dangerous. After a few seconds, you lose consciousness. It is basically threatening to your life. To defend effectively against such violent attacks, an effective technique must be applied without showing any hesitation. Firstly, it takes time to learn these practical countermeasures and skills. Secondly, whether people will be successful in defending themselves depends on the individual, the personal traits, actual experiences and the assessment of the specific situation.

I first considered adding pictures of techniques and ways to solve a broad spectrum of assaults and attacks by using self-defensive measures to this book. However, I came to the conclusion that even if pictures can be used to explain and illustrate certain aspects, it is still better to solemnly use general descriptions of martial arts schools and styles I know and have good experiences with. I think it is important to look for a good, experienced teacher and to have an "analogue" encounter with self-defensive skills as well as with yourself under these circumstances. By doing so, you can learn, practise, and integrate them better, so you are prepared and ready for actual situations.

I am going to describe some martial arts schools possessing specialities, which are very useful for self-defence. These schools again are divided into all kinds of branches and styles. Occasionally, different types of martial arts are combined and brought into a package, fitting certain target groups like women, juveniles, the elderly, social institutions, the army, police, security services etc. This opens opportunities and makes it altogether a bit more accessible for laypeople only wanting to be able to defend themselves or feel more secure without having to train every week. The techniques presented during such sessions for "laymen" are (or should be) in general easier to learn and pragmatic. It makes sense to think about the personal goals you want to achieve and what you want to use this technique for (street incidents or for your profession, with its typical tasks and inherent limitations to act). It is also important to consider how much time you have at your disposal and would like to invest. To feel more secure, self-confident and to be able to learn some tricks to fend off an attack is going to take little effort and investment of time. I would advise getting information about training offered at your work or private surroundings, giving it a try, and finding out what you need for yourself and what feels right.

Aikido is an inoffensive martial art. Its goal is not to harm but instead to lead the attacker with evasive moves adapted to the kind of attack into a space where he can calm himself down. The attacker is given the opportunity to have "second thoughts" and to decide to abstain from any further attacks. The aim is to gain time and enable the attacker to let off tension causing the aggressive attacks. However, if the attacker proceeds and does not calm down, Aikido has the means to apply defensive countermeasures against any further physical aggression effectively.

The word "Aikido" consists of three Japanese characters meaning harmony, universal energy and journey through life. It is often translated as "the way of unifying (with) life energy" or as "the way of harmonious spirit." Aikido techniques deliberately do not block an opponent's energy but are applied to regain control and use its force to our advantage. You can compare this principle with bamboo and how it bends in the wind but doesn't break. In comparison, a rigid tree would break under these circumstances since it does not have the characteristics to be able to go along and is relatively inflexible. You can also see the analogy with the going-along quality of attitude and its usefulness on some occasions.

Hapkido is a similar inoffensive style martial art originating from Korea. It also is composed out of many different types of sub-schools and styles. The character "hap" means "coordinated" or "joining"; "ki" describes internal energy, spirit, strength, or power; and "do" means "way" or "art", yielding a literal translation of "joining-energy-way". It is most often translated as "the way of coordinating energy", "the way of coordinated power" or "the way of harmony". The characteristics of this martial art are the application of joint locks, grappling and throwing techniques, as well as kicks, punches, and other striking attacks. The movements are circular and consist of flowing patterns. This way of moving has positive effects on our system, as it teaches us to control the body. Still, it also reinforces our body awareness and benefits finding a balance between body and mind.

Kyusho Jitsu from Japan is also known as the art of vital pressure points. This martial art is about the awareness of vital pressure points of the human body and how to use them for self-defence. Knowledge and principles from acupuncture and western neurology are brought together in this martial art. (Vital) pressure points are manipulated, often actually without using a lot of force, causing strong reactions within the attacker. This effect enables us to ward off attacks.

These techniques are very effective, especially when these pressure points are hit correctly. By manipulating the striking points, neurologic and physiologic processes within the human body are drastically influenced. This causes certain impairments depending on the kind of vital pressure point that has been struck. These include sudden bodily reflexes, pain, vertigo, loss of power and loss of consciousness. Physical condition and physical strength are not necessary to be able to defend yourself with these skills. Women, children, males or the elderly can all learn this art form and be successful. What is fundamental is the knowledge about the locations of the various points and how to manipulate them effectively, as well as having the right mindset. It is not advisable to train to hit these vital pressure points. However, what you can do is practice localising them and train your instincts and reflexes in case you are being attacked.

Chin NA or **Qui Na** originates from China and includes some impressive and very effective techniques. Some of them are used within other martial arts and fighting sports and are also taught within security services and in the army (in the Netherlands "back in the days" for sure). These skills are very effective in case somebody aggressively grabs hold of you. They are related to our natural instinctive reactions to physical attacks. By using them, you are enabled to regain control over the situation without using too much force, but with skills and techniques. Chin Na consists of a combination of surprise, joint locks, directed blows, grappling techniques, and applying pressure on vital pressure points. Hitting or applying pressure and blocking vital points (veins and arteries) and energetic areas (meridians) of the human body is known as **"Dim Mak"** and is a part of Chin Na, which is also thought to be the source of Martial Arts like Jiu-Jitsu and Aikido. Chin Na techniques are still developing, as many aspects can be creatively applied in various combinations.

I personally train people to use different and multiple elements of these main branches of martial arts. This has to do with my personal development and various professions I had, where experienced masters and trainers taught me these skills.

Final word

With this last chapter, I have come to the end of this book. I hope to have contributed positively to providing specific, compelling and valuable skills, and I hope you will feel more secure and self-confident when confronting aggressive people. It will take some time and effort to implement these principles and strategies in your professional and personal life. In the end, the content of this book should at least help you stay safe during the inevitable encounters with aggression.

Books

- Bach G.R. (2007), Keine Angst vor Aggression, Fischer Taschenbuch Verlag, Frankfurt am Main
- De Becker G. (1997), The Gift of Fear, Dell Publishing, New York
- Denker R. (1974), Angst und Aggression, W. Kohlhammer GmbH, Stuttgart
- Denker R. ((1976), Aggression im Spiel, Kohlhammer, Stuttgart
- Gilovich T. (2009), Heuristics and Biases, Cambridge University Press, New York
- Hopf H. (1998), Aggression in der analytischen Therapie mit Kindern und Jugendlichen, Vandenbroeck und Ruprecht, Göttingen
- Kaluza G. (2012), Gelassen und sicher im Stress, Springer Verlag, Berlin Heidelberg
- Ketelsen R. (2004), Seelische Krise und Aggressivität, Psychiatrie-Verlag GmbH, Bonn
- Klein G. (2004), The Power of Intuition, Currency Books, New York
- Kohut H. (1981), Die Heilung des Selbst, Suhrkamp Verlag, Frankfurt am Main
- Leary T. (1957) Interpersonal Diagnosis of Personality, Eugene OR
- Maltz, M. (1960), Psycho-Cybernetics, Pocket Books, New York
- Montaique E. (1997), The Encyclopedia of Dim-Mak, Paladin Press, Boulder
- Nolting H. (2005), Lernfall Aggression, Rowohlt Taschenbuch Verlag, Hamburg
- Redl F. (1986), Steuerung des aggressiven Verhaltens beim Kind, R. Piper Verlag GmbH & Co, K.G. München
- Redl F. (1966), When We Deal with Children, The Free Press, New York
- Reinisch S. (2012), Kyosho, Meyer & Meyer Verlag, Aachen
- Silva J. (1977), The Silva Mind Control Method, Pockets Books, New York
- Schranner M. (2005), Verhandeln im Grenzbereich, Econ Ullstein List Verlag GmbH. & Co KG, München
- Yang J. (2004), Analysis of Shaolin Chin Na, YMAA Publication, Boston

Additional templates for exercise one

General description of a situation:
Which feelings or internal sensations did this cause?
How did I react?

General description of a situation:
Which feelings or internal sensations did this cause?
How did I react?

Additional template for exercise four

General description of a situation:
What kind of feelings or internal sensations did this cause?
Observed behavioural characteristics of the aggressor:
Matching form of aggression:

Additional templates for exercise five

General description of a situation:
My attitude in this specific situation:
The attitude I find myself confronted with:
Are these attitudes complementary?
☐ yes   ☐ no

General description of a situation:
My attitude in this specific situation:
The attitude I find myself confronted with:
Are these attitudes complementary?
☐ yes   ☐ no

Room for personal notes: